crossing
the
desert

Learning to let go

see clearly

and live simply

SPIRITUAL GROWTH AND PROFESSIONAL DEVELOPMENT
BOOKS BY ROBERT J. WICKS

ROBERT J. WICKS

author of *Riding the Dragon*

crossing
the
desert

Learning to let go

see clearly

and live simply

SORIN BOOKS Notre Dame, Indiana

Excerpts from Robert Ellsberg, *The Saints' Guide to Happiness*, copyright © 2003 are used by permission of Farrar, Straus and Giroux.

Excerpts from Allen Jones, *Soul Making: The Desert Way of Spirituality*, copyright © 1985 are used by permission of HarperCollins Publishers.

Excerpts from Thomas Merton, *The Wisdom of the Desert*, copyright © 1960 by the Abbey of Gethsemani, Inc. are used by permission of New Directions Publishing.

Excerpts from Clark Strand, *The Wooden Bowl*, copyright © 1998 are used by permission of the author.

Excerpts from Robert J. Wicks, *Overcoming Secondary Stress in Medical and Nursing Practice*, copyright © 2005 are used by permission of Oxford University Press.

www.sorinbooks.com

ISBN-10 1-933495-08-1   ISBN-13 978-1-933495-08-8

Cover and text design by John Carson

Printed and bound in the United States of America.

CIP data is available from the Library of Congress.

She is energetic, bright, and captures your heart when you meet her.

Her comments and questions invariably make me smile.

Even at the age of three while watching me work in the garden

she would ask me deeply philosophical questions like,
"Why you do that Pop-Pop?"

~ For an amazing little girl—
   my granddaughter

Emily Dorothy Kulick

"Smooth seas do not make skillful sailors."

~African Proverb

"Where are the great and wise [persons] who do not merely talk about the meaning of life and the world but really possess it?"

~Carl Jung

CONTENTS

ACKNOWLEDGMENTS

I want to especially thank Mary Catherine Bunting for her support of me and my work. Due to her kindness, I am able to share this book with persons ministering in very difficult situations.

Wonderful stories bring principles and points to life. In this book, as in most of my work, I have integrated a number of experiences and illustrations. In addition to my own and those from other published sources, I want to thank Sheri Thornton Brown and Pamela S. Lowe, former students of mine, for allowing me to include several events from their personal journeys. They beautifully bring to light the specific challenges and joys many of us will encounter in life.

I would also like to acknowledge my long-time editor and friend Bob Hamma. Although in his role as Editorial Director of Sorin Books and Ave Maria Press there are many tasks for him to undertake, he gave a great deal of attention to this book so that my ideas would be expressed more clearly and not be lost unnecessarily. One of my goals in writing this book was to bring "desert wisdom" closer so that people could bring the themes of letting go and purity of heart home, and thus live their lives with greater simplicity and joy. Bob's editing has certainly brought me closer to my goal than I ever thought possible.

Finally, I would like to acknowledge my wife Michaele for her conversations, hours of editing early on when the manuscript was in its formative stage, and for her belief in what I was doing and why I was doing it. My words may be the lyrics of this book, but her inspiration, discussions, editing, and the model of her own life have provided the music of love that made the messages I have tried to convey as real and as meaningful as possible. Thank you, Michaele.

INTRODUCTION

*There are four questions and three steps that must be
encountered by anyone seriously interested in taking
a spiritual journey toward true inner freedom.*

*Paradoxically, nowhere does this occur
with greater potential for significant results
than in the deserts of our own life.*

*However, as sages have long taught, without the
right guidance and a receptive attitude, there is
also an equal danger that all will be lost.*

*The choice, fortunately or unfortunately,
depending upon our point of view, is ours.*

Desert Wisdom initially entered my life in a simple,
straightforward way. The subsequent encounter
with it, on the other hand, was a lot more intriguing and powerful for me.

I was first introduced to the history, spirituality, and
sayings of the desert fathers and mothers through the
writings of Thomas Merton. His book *The Wisdom of the
Desert* contained what I still believe is the best concise

introduction to the topic. His honesty and appreciation for the theme of ordinariness particularly intrigued me. He wrote:

> These monks insisted on remaining human and "ordinary." This may seem to be a paradox, but it is very important. If we reflect a moment, we will see that to fly into the desert in order to be extraordinary is only to carry the world with you as an implicit standard of comparison. The result would be nothing but self-contemplation and self-comparison with the negative standard of the world one had abandoned. Some of the monks of the desert did this, as a matter of fact: and the only fruit of their trouble was that they went out of their heads. The simple men who lived their lives out to a good old age among the rocks and sands only did so because they had come into the desert to be themselves, their ordinary selves, and to forget a world that divided them from themselves. There can be no other valid reason for seeking solitude or for leaving the world.
>
> [Moreover,] they knew that they were helpless to do any good for others as long as they floundered about in the wreckage. But once they got a foothold on solid ground, things were different.[1]

After reading Merton's introduction to the sayings of the early Desert Fathers and Mothers, I also read a wonderful work on the same topic by well-known spiritual writer and psychologist Henri Nouwen. In April 1984, when I went to visit him at Harvard to discuss my life and a new manuscript I was preparing on the theme of availability, I told him how taken I was with his treatment of the subject in *The Way of the Heart*.

He thanked me and said, "Well then maybe you would like this," and he gave me a copy of *Desert Wisdom*. It was a small collection of some of the sayings of the desert *abbas* and *ammas* translated and accompanied by Japanese brush paintings by Yushi Nomura. Henri was his professor and provided a short but solid introduction to the book. In it, his brief reflection contained a true appreciation of how we must learn to let go of what is unnecessary and untrue in ourselves. He made many compelling points like the following ones as to why these sayings, and the lives of those responsible for them, were no less relevant for us today in our seductive yet insecure times than they were many centuries ago:

> The world they tried to escape is the world in which money, power, fame, success, influence, and good connections are the ways to self esteem. It is the world that says, "You are what you have." This false identity gives the security and safety which we are searching for, but throws us in the spiral of a permanent desire for more—more money, more power and friends—in the illusion that one day we will arrive at that dream place where nobody and nothing can harm us. The hermits of the desert were deeply conscious of the fact that not only the society but also the church had been corrupted by this illusion. . . . They

escaped into the desert to free themselves from this compulsive self, to shake off the many layers of self-deception and reclaim their true self. . . . The way of the *abbas and ammas* of the desert makes it clear that finding our identity is not the simple result of having a new insight. Reclaiming our true self requires a total transformation. It requires a long and often slow process in which we enter more and more into the truth. . . . [Their stories and sayings] can speak directly to us, who live at least fifteen centuries after they were first written down. They do not require much explanation. What they do require is a spirit of discipleship, that is, a willingness to listen, to learn, and to be converted. . . .[2]

I continued to fathom the wisdom of the desert after this experience. Yet, for some reason I drifted away from using it to structure spiritual guidance for myself or as a way of responding to the questions from others about living peacefully in an anxious, fearful, and driven world. Then a strange thing happened. After Henri Nouwen died, he "returned" to my life again to direct me back to this literature in a way that graced me with a renewed appreciation and passion for it. He accomplished this not in person this time, but just as powerfully.

Henri died on September 21, 1996. Shortly after his death, Bill Sneck, a friend and colleague who knew how much I admired Henri, called and left a message. Bill, a sensitive and loving person, not only informed me of the details Nouwen's death, but offered consolation as well.

In response I went down into my basement library to look through Henri's writings. It was my way of grieving his loss.

As I thumbed through the pages of his books, I was amazed at how deeply I was touched by his death. I read a line here and a bracketed passage there. I was also surprised at how many of his books he had sent and inscribed for me. Then, I spied the *Desert Wisdom* book he had given me years back and my eyes fell on his simple inscription:

> *To Robert J. Wicks,*
> *in grateful memory of your visit.*
> *Joy and peace,*
> *Henri J. M. Nouwen,*
> *April 9, 1984*

After reflecting a bit in silence on this, I wondered: Why had I forgotten my deep love for (in Nouwen's words) "the spirit of discipleship" of the Desert Fathers and Mothers? How could I now use them more completely to help guide me in my own life as well as to assist others who sought my help? And finally, could I now glean the essential elements of a "desert spiritual apprenticeship" from a number of religious traditions to show me different ways to open up, let go, and be free to flow—rather than merely drift— with my life? Obviously, I felt deeply that the answer to these questions was yes, and this book is one of the results of that search.

Crossing The Desert is about the journey that all of us are called to take—*especially* when we feel lost, under great stress, or during times of desolation. And it is about discovering the true freedom we need to make it successfully.

As we journey through the deserts of life it is essential to know the right direction. Otherwise, we waste time wandering or, worse yet, get permanently lost. It is equally important to know what to bring. However, it is just as essential to know what not to bring, and what—or maybe whom—we need to let go of so that we are not unnecessarily pulled down or held back by what is destructive in life. How can we do this? Only with inner freedom.

The words of monk and well-known spiritual writer Thomas Merton can inspire us as we set out: "Happiness consists in finding out precisely what the 'one thing necessary' may be in our lives, and in gladly relinquishing all the rest. For then, by a divine paradox, we find that everything else is given us, together with the one thing we needed."[3]

Knowing this is the wisdom that the desert can teach us. Our task is to absorb this knowledge, and freedom is what comes with living out of it. Given each person's particular personality and circumstances, we must, as we will hear one of the ancient desert monks say "do the work [we] need to do first." While this is never easy, it is possible—even simple—and powerful, but only if we are willing to open ourselves, make the effort involved, and then let go. We have been given the grace to come this far. The choice about what to do now is ours.

There are two parts to this desert guide to inner freedom. First we will explore the practice of humility and the art of letting go. In today's climate of anxiety and arrogance, this classic virtue of humility is no less pertinent for a person wishing to live simply and peacefully than it was in the turbulent fourth century. We will explore the narrow gates of passion and knowledge through which we must pass on the way to humility. We will also look at four types of friends we need for our journey and the important roles our friends can play in helping us become humble. The last chapter in this section focuses on gratefulness, the virtue that helps us see clearly and maintain perspective.

Part two continues to reflect on the sayings of the Desert Fathers and Mothers and parallel themes from modern psychology and spirituality as guidance for addressing four central questions that arise during everyone's journey toward inner freedom. They are the questions that must also be confronted—especially in the deserts of our lives— as part of the ongoing process of letting go. Only then can we fill ourselves with what, paradoxically, both satisfies us and allows us to still remain spiritually hungry, open, fluid, and free. As we struggle to let go of what burdens us and limits us, we will look at the many ways we can feed our souls with the food that both satisfies us and makes us long for more. We will explore what it means to become both a "desert apprentice" and a spiritual mentor, if and when others turn to us for help. The significance of this focus is twofold. First, it recognizes the need for guidance in our own lives so we can "let go" without losing our way. Yet, just as important during a time when the need for good mentors is so great, it raises our awareness to the necessity of being a healing presence to others as well.

Our role as guide can be very important to those around us. It may be informal, simple, and a good deal of the time offered not so much in the words we say as in the listening spirit we provide. However, it is a key element not only to being compassionate, but also—in some mysterious way—to feeling fulfilled ourselves. As a result, compassion joined with spiritual wisdom forms a circle of grace in our own lives that must never be broken. On the one hand, without compassionate activity on our part there is a great danger that the search for ways to let go and have inner freedom can silently slip into quietism or hedonism. On the other hand, without spiritual wisdom, our compassion may turn out to be erratic, self-serving, or undisciplined, and lead to burnout and disillusionment.

Instead, the goal of *Crossing The Desert*, in drawing upon fourth-century desert wisdom and the contemporary figures who follow or parallel that wisdom, is to provide proven guidance on how to let go and live with a refreshing sense of freedom in the world. This in turn enables us to help others who interact with us also to be free. The desire for anything less is insufficient. To be concerned only with self-improvement and personal security or peace is to distort the very heart of the wisdom of the desert. The fruit of desert wisdom should, in fact, help us let go of what is unnecessary so we can be filled with good things in ways that will enhance rather than subdue our own freedom or that of others.

Finally, the short closing chapter focuses on the three necessary steps that each of us must take, when the time is right, if we wish to have the inner freedom to flow with, rather than drift through, our lives. It is designed to demonstrate how letting go creates in us the qualities of single-heartedness, purity of heart, and peace (*quies*). Letting go not only brings them to us, but also to those with whom we come into contact. All of this is possible *now* and at each subsequent stage of life.

one

LET THE DESERT
TEACH YOU

The desert has always been a place of fascination, awe, and fear. Even today, when we encounter an actual desert, its immense physical harshness quickly puts our lives in perspective. As William Langewiesche revealed in his book *Sahara Unveiled*:

> [The desert] is the earth stripped of its gentleness, a place that consumes the careless and the unlucky. . . . The Sahara has horizons so bare that drivers mistake stones for diesel trucks, and so lonely that migrating birds land beside people just for the company. The certainty of such sparseness can be a lesson. I lay in Algiers in a hotel in a storm, thinking there is no better sound than the splash of rain.[4]

In an encounter with such barrenness, we become truly grateful for the little things that we often take for granted but which actually make life good. From a spiritual vantage point Alan Jones adds:

> The desert does strange things to the way one sees. It plays tricks with the imagination and, at the same time, intensifies and magnifies experiences. The hot sun and the apparent deadness of the desert clarify one's mind and reorder one's priorities. It is easy to see why codes of hospitality are strictly adhered to in this part of the world. Hospitality is a matter of mutual survival. It didn't take me long to realize what most mattered in all the world. Heat, dust, and loneliness made me appreciate our need for three simple things: food, shelter, and companionship.[5]

So, in the desert, an opportunity to gain a new perspective and a unique appreciation for what is truly important is joined by a radically different sense of what relationship, hospitality, and compassion should mean in our lives. Is it any wonder then, that the desert would be an ideal metaphor for the challenging times in life to remind us of the need to let go of all that is incomplete and unnecessary in us?

The impact of the desert goes beyond almost any possible experience of silence, solitude, and deprivation. In a letter to her father, Gertrude Bell, a contemporary of Lawrence of Arabia, dramatically describes this:

> [The] endless desert. . . . Shall I tell you my chief impression—the silence. It is like the silence of mountain tops, but more intense, for there you know the sound of wind and far way water and falling ice and stones; there is a sort of echo of sound there, you know it Father. But here *nothing*.[6]

Yet, it is in this very atmosphere of "nothingness" fed by the silence and solitude that we, when we must enter our own deserts, are given the unsought opportunity to re-evaluate our lives and potentially experience true inner freedom—*if* we have the right guidance. We can find such guides in the fourth-century desert monks and nuns.

When we find ourselves on a desert journey, who better to turn to for guidance than the ancient disciples of the desert who have physically and/or spiritually entered into these barren areas, only to emerge with wisdom to share. They learned to live more simply, gratefully, and completely. So too can we. With their guidance we can be released from unnecessary worries and tendencies to travel down fruitless paths.

We know them today as the fourth-century Christian *ammas* and *abbas*. They were people who drew inspiration from Moses, Elijah, John the Baptist, and Jesus, the desert dwellers who lived before them. These prophetic figures knew much about what lies at the core of life. *Abbas* and *ammas* were true spiritual apprentices who appreciated the need to let go of whatever may be squeezing the air out of life either spiritually or psychologically. They were also able to welcome that which would replenish one's soul and foster inner freedom.

These fourth-century pilgrims were a fascinating, unusual, and loose community of people who sought "simply" to be themselves and not fall prey to the culture of greed, power, and preoccupation with one's image and achievements. They knew about the illusion of control and that security based on anything less than trust in God was pure folly. They also fully understood and deeply embraced the belief that when we add the humility of the desert (what we might call "ordinariness" today) to sound practical knowledge, the result can be true wisdom.

Their commitment to what is true and good led them to spare no effort in their search for themselves and God. Their commitment to live more authentic lives drove them to let go of current social norms and follow uncharted ways to find and embrace the truth. Because they succeeded in doing this, their lives became transparent, and in that transparency they were able to offer others a pure space, uncontaminated by insecurity, self-interest, pride, or any other number of inner "demons," as they called them, that are often left unnoticed and unexpelled from most people's lives. They were persons without guile, transparent, *free*. Unlike much of the world then—and now—they were not held captive by worldly values, anxieties, or fears; they, perhaps more than any other group we could learn from, appreciated the beauty and freedom of *ordinariness*.

The Desert Fathers and Mothers emerged at a time when Christianity was in danger of losing its prophetic character. The Roman Emperor Constantine had just converted to Christianity, and with the proclamation of the Edict of Milan in 313, it was no longer illegal to be a Christian. The church and the temporal order were reconciled. One might say that the church was becoming domesticated. It no longer existed as a challenge to the Empire. Christians no longer feared persecution and began to become comfortable with the status quo.

Happily, there were some Christians who recognized that this process presented a new danger to faith: secularization and compromise. Following the example of the first hermit, Anthony of Egypt, these men and women took a very dramatic step: they left the cities and towns and went out to the deserts that surrounded them. There they began to live in silence and solitude. In doing so they set a dramatic example. They embraced what came to be called the "white martyrdom" of asceticism in imitation of those who were put to death for their faith in the "red martyrdom" of the Roman persecution. For later Christians who followed them into the "wilderness," either in fact or in spirit, they have shown the way to the very heart of discipleship and demonstrated that to embrace the desire to find God also requires that we find ourselves. The Desert Fathers and Mothers asked for the grace to let go of the illusions and delusions upon which their identity had previously been based. They wished only to discover how to be themselves—to be ordinary.

Along the way these courageous people discovered that the journey into the desert was just the beginning. The longest and most difficult journey was the journey inward. Centuries later, Teresa of Avila taught explicitly that we find God by uncovering our own true selves; and it is in the search for God that we can better discover who we are. These early Christians were learning this through their experience and have passed it on to us in their wise stories and sayings. Their appreciation for ordinariness enabled them to realize intuitively what theologians call "the divinization of the human person." Contemporary psychologists describe this as having a healthy self-esteem. Such a person is not dramatically swayed by the opinions or reactions of others.

Such ordinariness and transparency on the part of these desert dwellers contains within it a humility that directs us to center our faith in God alone and nothing less. The result: a deep sense of peace in times of turmoil. Because these desert dwellers were able to let go of their familiar world and take Christ as their guide to something new, their life was countercultural. Consequently, they weren't pulled in by the anxieties of the world, but could stand within their troubles in a way that allowed them to be of help to others too. They also modeled a lesson that would pervade Franciscan spirituality much later on: There is nothing so strong as gentleness and nothing so gentle as real strength. Having a better sense of themselves and God enabled them to be compassionate in a freer, more natural, and kinder way. It wasn't that there was never a time for being firm. But their self-knowledge and awareness of their own frailties gave rise to a special sensitivity to individual situations and an appreciation of the value of pacing with respect to spiritual growth. A simple desert story illustrates this well.

> A few of the brothers came to see Abba Poemen.
> They said to him, "Tell us what to do when we see brothers dozing during prayer. Should we pinch them to help them stay awake?"
> The elder said to them, "Actually what I would do if I saw a brother sleeping is to put his head on my knees and let him rest."[7]

The Desert Fathers and Mothers followed Jesus' example of going out to the desert to hear the word of God, to encounter temptations (Mt 4:1, Mk 1:2, Lk 4:1), and to "come away to some lonely place all by yourself and rest for a while" (Mk 6:31). As Thomas Merton recognized, the flight of these early pilgrims to the desert was "a refusal to be content with arguments, concepts, and technical verbiage. They sought a way to God that was uncharted and freely chosen, not inherited from others who had mapped it out beforehand. They sought a God whom they alone could find, not one who was given in a set, stereotyped form by somebody else."[8]

Although their actions may seem extraordinary and be impossible for us, they still have a lot to teach us about being ordinary. The desert was a place where it was difficult to hide from the most basic demands of ordinary Christian life. Their struggle to live their faith to the fullest offers us a model for fashioning our own ordinary way, a way that imitates theirs because it too is uncharted yet freely chosen. As they sought to discover both God and their true selves, unexpected graces emerged. By appreciating their own ordinariness they were able to become free. And they became strong enough to help others experience the simple presence of God in themselves. They became gentle and strong enough to be truly compassionate.

Only with wisdom of this sort can we live authentically with ourselves, others, and God. Given this, the goal of this book is to provide a sense of how obscure women and men of the fourth century, along with some of the other most beloved spiritual writers of our time, offer us the wisdom of the desert to free us from the chains of our modern insecurities and attachments. However, the wisdom gleaned from the desert is not meant simply to be something that we read about. Instead, each lesson strikes a personal chord and needs to be reflected upon and applied in some way to one's own life. If it is to have real meaning, each lesson must be *lived*—personally and completely.

The lessons that follow cannot be left in someone else's desert. Otherwise, all this wisdom will remain on an intellectual shelf to be admired from afar but not fully embraced where it counts the most, in daily life. True insight only occurs when the head and the heart come together and lead to changes in the way we live. Without change we cannot gain new insight. No change, no insight. Real change requires humility, openness, and—most of all—a willingness to act on what we know and to admit what we don't.

As a therapist, if an alcoholic comes to see me and he gains mere knowledge about his condition, there is no real change, only information. As a result, all we have now is an enlightened alcoholic! To truly change, the lesson must be experienced deeply. Then, and only then, a new life of greater perspective and true ordinariness can be experienced and shared with others in a way that will have real impact.

As Merton notes about the fourth-century desert *ammas* and *abbas*:

> We cannot do exactly what they did. But we must be as thorough and as ruthless in our determination to break all spiritual chains and cast off the domination of alien compulsions, to find our true selves, to discover and develop our inalienable spiritual liberty and use it to build, on earth, the Kingdom of God. This is not the place in which to speculate what our great and mysterious vocation might involve. That is still unknown. Let it suffice for me to say that we need to learn from these men [and women] of the fourth

century how to ignore prejudice, defy compulsion, and strike out fearlessly into the unknown.[9]

At this point, I think a desert story can better describe what I am saying and, in turn, point to the *abbas'* and *ammas'* approach to reflecting over and practicing what is contained in the remainder of this book on the theme of letting go.

> A young man came to see an Abba to speak about how to meditate and live a simple, reflective life. But rather than being humble, open, tentative, and patient, he excitedly started to speak about things he hadn't either tried or experienced himself.
>
> In response, the old man looked at him gently and said in a clear, level voice: "You have not found a boat, put what you own into it, or pushed off from the shore, but you seem to have already arrived at the town on the opposite bank!
>
> "Well, *do the work you need to do first.* Then, you will come to the point you are speaking about to me now."[10]

part one

To Embrace the Freedom that Humility Offers

SEEK WHAT IS ESSENTIAL

Ask most people what they want today and their answer is often very simple: a little peace and joy in their lives. In search of this, some shuttle from spirituality to spirituality looking for the way to find it. Others dig in their "psychological heels" and pull dogmatic theological tenets over their heads in an effort to shield themselves from change and insecurity. Their hope is that these anchors will provide the security they desperately desire. But, they never do.

One ancient group, however, saw the world's insecurities and lack of values as a wake-up call to let go of what was causing their anxiety. For them being troubled wasn't simply the result of encountering something disturbing that needed to be conquered or removed. Instead, anxiety was a signal and an opportunity to gain *a new sense of perspective* in order to determine or rediscover what is essential in life. To their mind, whatever effort it took to experience true inner freedom and gain this new way of seeing was worth it. They wanted to free themselves from unnecessary worry and worldly snares through a new centered attitude and, in turn, experience the real fruits of Jesus' words, "if your eye is good, your whole body will be good" (Mt 6:24).

Our goal can be the same. Namely, we can see life differently by seeking humility, or as the Desert Fathers and Mothers called it, "purity of heart." As Thomas Merton points out, "purity of heart [is a] clear unobstructed vision of the true state of affairs, an intuitive grasp of one's own inner reality as anchored, or rather lost, in God through Christ."[11]

Buddhists may refer to this state as "unobstructed vision." In the *Upanishads*, Hindus describe a similar experience as "turning around in one's seat of consciousness." Dynamically oriented psychotherapists interested in unconscious forces may seek to approximate a version of this awareness of clarity by helping their clients make the unknown known. They seek to enable them to become conscious of their resistances to change, develop good self-knowledge based on increased awareness of what were once unconscious forces, or reach a level of maturity at which they have "a less fractious ego." Despite the help psychology can provide us in our search for inner freedom, purity of heart in the spiritual sense requires more than psychological insight or maturity. It involves a true *conversion*, the fruits of which include the inner peace of letting go of unnecessary worry and attachments by opening ourselves to God in a new and radical way.

Before we can follow in the path of those who have sought and found the freedom that accompanies purity of heart, we must first be honest and humble enough to appreciate that we are not free now. Humility must be at the very core of a desert wisdom outlook, attitude, or perspective. For example, Abba Anthony, the Father of the Desert, said, "I saw all the snares that the enemy spreads out over the whole world and I said, groaning, 'What can get me through such snares?' Then I heard a voice saying to me, 'Humility.'"[12]

In addition, it is necessary not only to see ourselves for who we are (with both our gifts and our growing edges). But it is just as important to take the *actions* to let go of what has captured our hearts, preoccupied us unnecessarily, and made us insecure and anxious. The fourth-century Desert Fathers and Mothers sought true inner freedom and peace and were willing to pay the price for it. Fortunately for us, they left guidance in the form of stories and sayings for those who wish to follow in their path. How they followed their desire to let go and have the one essential thing they needed in their hearts to "find the simple truth about who we are and how we ought to live"[13] is described in the conversations between these *abbas* and *ammas* and their disciples.

These stories, referred to as "the sayings" have lasted for centuries because they contain concrete wisdom that has remained relevant for all people down through the ages. Such wisdom can provide important direction for us now when there seems to be few people who have true peace and joy in their hearts or are able to share this beautiful inner space with others. By absorbing the knowledge and ethos of the *ammas* and *abba*s and those who parallel or imitate much of their spiritual paradigm, we can join with spiritual seekers through the centuries who have applied the wisdom and guidance of these ancient sayings in their own time.

A Few Words about the Sayings

The sayings have endured through the centuries for a number of reasons. In *The Word and the Desert*, the most truly comprehensive treatment of desert wisdom I have seen to date, Douglas Burton-Christie points out several reasons for their long life:

> [I]t is commonly understood in the desert that one did not speak apart from an inspiration from God, nor did one convey such a word to a listener unless that person showed a willingness to put the word into action. The sayings emerged and gained currency as words of power, life, and salvation addressed to particular persons in concrete situations.[14]

[T]he sayings are very practical in character and encourage imitation rather than reflection and speculation. The editor [of the sayings] has emphasized this by noting that the primary purpose of the sayings is not to "teach" or "instruct" the ones seeking a word but rather to "help" them.

Almost always there is found within the elder's exposition a challenge of some kind.

The overarching goal of the sayings was to help people seek what those in the desert sought: purity of heart and its primary fruit, *quies*. To quote Merton again with respect to this central theme:

The fruit of [purity of heart] was *quies*: "rest." Not rest of the body, nor even fixation of the exalted spirit upon some point or summit of light. The Desert Fathers were not, for the most part, ecstatics. Those who were have left some strange and misleading stories behind them to confuse the true issue. The "rest" which these men sought was simply the sanity and poise of being that no longer has to look at itself because it is carried away by the perfection of freedom that is in it. And carried where? Wherever Love itself, or the Divine Spirit, sees fit to go. Rest, then, was a kind of simple no-whereness and no-mindedness that had lost all preoccupation with a false or limited "self." At peace in the possession of a sublime "Nothing" the spirit laid hold, in secret, upon the "All"—without trying to know what it possessed.[15]

Unlearning

To seek the freedom that humility offers, we first have
to appreciate that our vision is not clear now. Instead,
although we may not readily see it, our soul is heavy, and
our psychological arms are full of so much that is unnecessary and harmful to our sense of simplicity and peace. We
need to become aware of, and even disgusted by, this terrible reality. When we do, we will know deep in our hearts
that there is a serious need for unlearning and emptiness.
This is essential before we can welcome the fresh wisdom
that will set us free from the cultural and unconscious
chains that are binding us. Once again, as Douglas Burton-
Christie writes of one of the early Fathers of the Church,

> For [John Cassian], the problem with the old
> learning was at least in part psychological: it
> prevented the mind from absorbing the new ethos of
> the Scriptures. . . . There was a clear sense among the
> educated ones who came to the desert that learning
> would have to start over in this place.[16]

But how do we start over? Or, more specifically, what
are the essential questions that must be asked and confronted in life if we wish to let go of all that is unnecessary in our desire for purity of heart? Many questions
can be posed in response to this. Still, as will be discussed
later in the book, there are four central ones that I believe
desert apprentices then and now must confront. This
must be done if we are to really let go of everything that

is troubling and misdirected in ourselves so we can be free—not just free for ourselves but for those who count on us as well. This does not mean that we will never be without pain. No one will ever be in that state. It means being free from the common, yet unnecessary, suffering that overshadows our days that, with some serious attention, can be discarded so in its place we can open space for creative and generous pursuits.

For some, the concept of letting go is truly an attractive pursuit. Yet, approaching these questions honestly and fully will reveal that while living with such an attitude and spiritual center may be basically simple, it is still not easy to accomplish. At each step of the way and at each stage of life, our challenge will be to recall the question: Am I still truly serious about seeking what will free me? Using another scriptural metaphor, the pearl of great price is worth everything, but are we willing to pay this cost? People say they are willing, at least in theory or in their desire to do this. But actually taking the steps that are needed to commit oneself to such a serious search is obviously quite another thing!

Once when I was in Corpus Christi, Texas, for a meeting, I met a former student of mine. He now had a leadership position, and I was interested in how he was faring in this new role. He suggested dinner, and later that night we sat down for a wonderful meal and great conversation. At one point, he surprised me with the comment: "I'll never forget one of the points that you made in class." Intrigued,

I asked him which point made such an impression on him. He smiled and replied, "You told us that we could have peace if we wanted it. Then, after a short pause you added, 'as long as that was *all* we wanted.'"

The difference between true passionate intent that leads to action and mere fantasy that results in inaction is a distinction that all major religions make when addressing the topics of letting go or the freedom and peace that true spiritual practice can bring. Donald Brazier, in his insightful work *Zen Therapy*, describes this distinction from a Buddhist perspective:

> Shakyamuni [Buddha] wanted to know why there was so much trouble in the world, and he gave up a kingdom to find out. We also inwardly long for an answer, but, in most cases, are unwilling to give up our kingdom. We have mastered many techniques for keeping our question bound and gagged. We coat our grit [suffering or bitterness] in plastic so as not to feel its sharp edges. Plastic does not work for long, however. The grit demands real pearl. The advance of life, again and again, inevitably, exposes the inadequacy of our efforts to cover up the trouble inside.

> These days, at such times, we are apt to seek out a therapist to, if I may change the metaphor, help us get the dragon back into its cave. Therapists of many schools will oblige in this, and we will thus be returned to what Freud called "ordinary unhappiness" and, temporarily, heave a sigh of relief, our repressions working smoothly once again. Zen by

contrast, offers dragon-riding lessons, for the few who are sufficiently intrepid.[17]

Such dragon-riding lessons are also contained in the sayings of the fourth-century Desert Fathers and Mothers. They guide, nurture, and challenge us as we seek to embrace questions that, maybe for years, we have ignored, skirted, or set aside when they arose. In place of covering, avoiding, or running away, if we really wish the transparency and purity of heart that will set us free, we can address a number of serious questions that are implicitly raised when we look at the sayings. For our purposes here, as I noted earlier, I have made four of them explicit as a way of structuring their challenges in a way that is still very relevant for us today. Before we face these questions, there is a desert spirit or virtue we must explore. Without this essential ingredient our desire to respond to the four questions offered in the next part as well as attempting to absorb the ethos of the rest of the book would be futile.

three

ENTER THROUGH
THE NARROW GATES

All of us must pass through three "psycho-spiritual gates" on the journey to a full life. If we wish to be open to and benefit from all we experience—including the painful deserts—we must learn to walk through each one. If we don't, we consign ourselves to an existence that is one of merely going through the motions each day.

The first gate is passion. Passion is not unnecessary exuberance. Rather, it is a sense of commitment, faithfulness, and appreciation of the gift of life. It is not dimmed by failure because passion is not based on success. Instead it is fired by a spiritual sense of awe for what life can be when it is touched by courage, openness, and gratitude for all we have been given.

The revered rabbi, Abraham Joshua Heschel, had such a sense of passion. It pervaded his life and even his road to death. This is evidenced in the following story by his former student, longtime friend, colleague, and fellow rabbi, Samuel Dresner:

> Several years before Abraham Heschel's death in 1972, he suffered a near fatal heart attack from which he never fully recovered. I traveled to his apartment in New York to see him. He had gotten out of bed for the first time to greet me, and was sitting in the living room when I arrived, looking weak and pale. He spoke slowly and with some effort, almost in a whisper. I strained to hear his words.
>
> "Sam," he said, "when I regained consciousness, my first feelings were not of despair or anger. I felt only gratitude to God for my life, for every moment I had lived. I was ready to depart. 'Take me, O Lord,' I thought, 'I have seen so many miracles in my lifetime.'"
>
> Exhausted by the effort, he paused for a moment, then added: "That is what I meant when I wrote [in the preface to my book of Yiddish poems]: 'I did not ask for success; I asked for wonder. And You gave it to me.'"[18]

Now, that's passion!

The second gate is knowledge. True knowledge can shield us from unnecessary mistakes in nurturing our inner life, as well as that of our family, friends, and others who seek our help when they are lost, confused, or in a "spiritual desert." Motivation is important but it is not enough. Passion helps us to start the car and be open to the adventure of the trip. But it also helps if we *know* how to drive!

To keep a healthy perspective in life we need to have both the psychological and spiritual wisdom that the different world religions offer us. Such wisdom helps one to differentiate between unnecessary suffering on the one hand, and the kind of pain that must be faced rather than defended against or avoided on the other. Good knowledge, like healthy food, is necessary for living. Consequently living by the principles of self-care and maintaining a healthy perspective are two things we naturally seek each day. We need this knowledge. However, it is the third and final gate that will determine the true *quality* of our life.

The third gate has been the focus of our reflections thus far: humility. It the narrowest one of all. Humility is the ability to fully appreciate our innate gifts and our current "growing edges" in ways that enable us to learn, act, and flow with our lives as never before. Prior to this important passage we may be drained by defensiveness or wander in our own desert chasing a false image of self that has nothing to do with who we are really meant to be.

Most of us know that at some point we need to go through the gate of humility. That is not the problem. The issue is that we are often unaware of the fact that we have actually stopped being humble and, in the process, have lost our sense of perspective and gratitude. If we are lucky, something wakes us up to this fact, even if rudely. The following story shared with me by a Franciscan priest illustrates this point quite well:

> I had a dream that death
> Came the other night,
> And Heaven's gate swung wide open.
>
> With kindly grace
> An angel ushered me inside;
> And there to my astonishment
> Stood folks I had known on earth
> And some I had judged
> And labeled unfit and of little worth.
>
> Indignant words rose to my lips,
> But were never set free;
> for every face showed stunned surprise,
> Not one expected *me.*
>   —Anonymous

With humility, knowledge is transformed into wisdom. Such wisdom then ultimately leads us to open up new space within ourselves where we, as well as others, can experience true freedom and love. Humility allows us to be transparent. It is for this reason that humility is so important. So much unnecessary worry and stress can be avoided if we treasure this gift. A dialogue from a collection of classic stories and teachings of the early Christian writers (*Patrologia Latina* and *Patrologia Graeca*) told by the *ammas* and *abbas* of the fourth-century desert in Persia and northern Africa illustrates this. It is told from the vantage point of persons totally dedicated to living a full, meditative life of inner peace, humility, and unselfconscious compassion—a place all of us should seek to be.

> The devil appeared to a Desert Father, in the disguise of an angel of the Lord, and said to him, "I am the angel Gabriel and I have been sent to you."
>
> However, the Father softly responded, "See if you are not being sent to someone else. I certainly do not deserve to have an angel sent to me."
>
> Immediately, the devil disappeared.[19]

This is the kind of natural attitude we need so that we can pass through the third gate. It will also allow us to have the perspective, peace, and joy that come when we know and value our ordinary, transparent selves without wasting the energy it takes to add or subtract anything from who we really are. Humility is an *essential* ingredient in life because it provides a *kenosis*, an emptying of the self—the very desert spirit of letting go about which this book is written. At its core, humility dramatically opens up beautiful space in our inner life:

- a space for simplicity amidst the complex demands of both home and office;
- a space for solitude to listen to the messages of our quiet spirit lest they be drowned out by the day's noise;
- a space for pacing ourselves while resisting the lure of speed and new technology;
- a space for gratefulness and giftedness in a world filled with a sense of entitlement;
- a space for honesty and clarity rather than spinning the truth to our own advantage;
- a space for real relationships in place of mere manipulation of others;
- a space for restraint instead of instant gratification and aggression;
- a space for doubt and deeper questions rather than filling our selves with false certainty and pat answers;
- a space for reflection so that compassion doesn't lead to undisciplined activism;
- a space for generosity where previously only strident self-interest stood;
- a space for transparency where opaque defensiveness is our normal rule;

- a space for sound self-respect in lieu of inordinate self-doubt or unbridled self-assurance;

- a space for intrigue or curiosity about our actions and motivations so we don't wander down the blind alleys of projection or self-condemnation;

- a space for forgiveness so we don't fall prey to rigidity and self-righteousness;

- a space for what will always be true rather than solely having an interest in what is currently in vogue; and

- a space for the courage needed to be ordinary instead of wasting all of our time chasing after what we believe will make us someone special.

Yes, it is the ability to empty ourselves that creates new inner space in our lives for the surprising remarkable gifts of humility.

Humility in Silence and Solitude

Anthony de Mello, an Indian Jesuit priest and psychologist, relates the following classic dialogue between a spiritual master and a novice disciple:

"Why is everyone here so happy except me?"

"Because they have learned to see goodness and beauty everywhere."

"Why don't I see goodness and beauty everywhere?"

"Because you cannot see outside of you what you fail to see inside."[20]

When we sit in silence and solitude, we expect a sense of peace. At first, this is what happens. We are so glad that we have entered a space where we are free from the fast pace and tensions of life. However, if we sit long enough we eventually get uncomfortable, even anxious. We get ideas. We remember things we must do. We want to get up and write these down, make phone calls, or pick up a book.

If we resist such actions, the next phase of the silent period begins. During this period, we hear the noise that is going on in our belief system. Like a radio turned onto "scan," our mind moves from different events—both recent and remote—that have emotional power. Hurts, shame, the silver casket of nostalgia, proud moments, anger, resentment, all come to the surface. Depending upon our personality style, we respond to them with projection, self-condemnation, or discouragement that we are still dealing with these issues and old agendas. This is a crucial point on the road to both humility and a spirit of letting go.

Buddhists would gently suggest that we keep our seat and let the stories of the past move through us, acting as though it were about someone else. No judgment. No excuses. No blame. Just watch. From a Christian perspective, Amma Syncletica, a fourth-century desert dweller, would also offer encouragement by putting it this way:

> In the beginning of prayer there is struggle and lots of work for those who come near to God. But after that, there is indescribable joy. It is just like building a fire: at first it is smoky and your eyes water, but later you get the desired result. Thus we ought to light the divine fire in ourselves with tears and effort.[21]

From a psychological, rather than purely spiritual perspective, what happens in the silence is that we create an opportunity for the irrational but as yet undisputed thoughts about ourselves and the world to surface. Such thoughts usually remain in hiding because we don't like them. As soon as they surface, we want to avoid or justify them in some way—even when, maybe especially when, we are alone.

This is unfortunate because they are the front line of deeper irrational beliefs that are crippling us. In therapy or in spiritual mentoring, we begin to see these irrational beliefs as such once we have enough trust to share everything that comes to mind. However, think how wonderful it would be if, in the search for our true selves and the desire to experience the inner space offered by humility, we could also do this *with ourselves* through regular, even brief, periods of silence and solitude.

Lacking opportunities for such uncoverings and debriefings with ourselves, such thoughts are left to attack us at night and keep us awake. They haunt us when events occur in our lives that make us uncomfortable. They pain us when we feel we have done the wrong thing or have been mistreated by others. But such suffering at those times, in those ways, unfortunately doesn't teach us anything of worth. What a waste.

On the other hand, if we intentionally make the space for—in Buddhist imagery—these "unruly unconscious children" to run around in our consciousness, then our silence and solitude become a classroom where we learn what is driving us . . . usually in the *wrong* direction. Also, as was implied by Amma Syncletica in her above admonishment, we will also have a chance, once the dust of delusion settles, to have a space within to be freer in life.

If we see our growing edges clearly—without excuses, inordinate self-blame, or discouragement (maybe because we have not improved quickly enough)—then the energy usually employed to defend or attack ourselves can be more profitably channeled into learning how we might better enjoy the life we have been given. In addition, our life, and the way we honestly view it, can provide a clearer path in our relationships as well.

Opening ourselves up to past agendas, distorted thoughts, hurtful ideas, and false beliefs that lurk below the surface and rise into the vacuum we have created in silence can teach us much. We just need to give ourselves the space to allow these unexamined memories and perceptions to surface so we can see, examine, and address them with love and understanding. The brilliant analyst Alfred Adler once pointed out that children are great observers but poor interpreters. The un-worked-through interpretations we also made as children that remain within our unconscious and preconscious are really no different. We must meet them and allow them to tell their stories if we are to find the truth.

Silence and solitude will help us to delve into the darkness in our inner life (the area some would refer to as our soul) to accomplish this. However, as we will soon recognize, we still cannot find the truth and the freedom of humility by ourselves in quiet meditation, although this is a necessary step in the intriguing process of self-understanding and appreciation. For a fuller self-understanding and appreciation of what humility might mean to us in concrete, practical ways that can be transformative, we will also need direction from the different "voices" present in our trusted circle of friends.

four

LISTEN TO FRIENDS

The reappraisal that silence and solitude provide on the journey to humility is further strengthened by the relationships we have. Although time alone in reflection and meditation offers the opportunity for the honesty that forms a basis for humility, without additional outside voices to challenge, encourage, tease, and call us to be all we can be, it is still easy to delude ourselves. For this reason, I suggest that everyone should ensure that they can listen to these four "voices" within their circle of friends so they don't fall prey to the dangerous extremes of inordinate self-confidence on the one hand, or undue self-doubt on the other.[22]

The first voice is one we don't like; it is the *prophet*. No one likes the prophet. As Henry Thoreau once said, "if you see someone coming to do good for you . . . run for your life!" The prophet is the person who challenges us to continually look at ourselves. She helps us appreciate that the congruence between our words and behavior makes all the difference. Yet, often we are not able to see this ourselves.

One time an Irish priest and I sat down for breakfast with a self-proclaimed peace activist, a would-be prophet. The peace activist was very intense, and while I was with him I felt no sense of peace myself. As a matter of fact, every time he said "pass the sugar!" it was as though he were announcing an incoming nuclear attack. Finally, when the peace activist got up to get another cup of coffee, the Irish priest put down his spoon and looked at me a bit dazed. In response, I said, "What is it Sean?" And he said in reply, "Glory be to God, Robert. Every time that boy speaks about peace, he scares the hell out of me!"

Unlike the intense, young peace activist, real prophets ask us the important questions: What voices are guiding you in life? Who from early life or contemporary culture is pulling your strings? Humility does not simply involve poking a hole in our own inflated egos where necessary, it also helps us step back from blindly following the messages we receive from others. Prophets help us take stock of how we are living and take personal responsibility for our decisions. They model for us the need to gain a sense of distance from our own lives. No matter how important our role in our family or society, it is very easy to get over involved in our inner self and lose perspective. The following reflection by Harvard psychiatrist Robert Coles on his initial contact with peace activist Dorothy Day illustrates this:

> My mother was no stranger to the Catholic Worker movement, although she was Episcopalian in background. She had been urging Dorothy on me all my life. My father was Jewish and Catholic both, but he was much less interested in Dorothy Day.
>
> I was in medical school in Columbia and not enjoying it much. Kept complaining about it to my mother, and she said that what I needed was to go down and work at a soup kitchen for Dorothy Day instead of complaining. I understood what my mother was getting at. She used to say that there are things more important than the troubles you are having, and there are people who might help you to understand that and especially help you get some distance from your complaining and from the rather privileged position of being a medical student. The long and the short of it is, I eventually went down and met Dorothy Day.[23]

The second essential voice or friend for the inner journey of humility is the *cheerleader*. If we just have prophets we will burn out. If we just have "cheerleaders" we will be narcissistic. We need a balance of both. But we do need cheerleaders to support us through the tough times so we don't hear praise as a whisper and negativity as thunder.

The cheerleader helps us see the positive truth about ourselves now and the potential we have in the future.

This ensures that our humility doesn't become distorted into self-abasement or lead to an avoidance of taking our proper place at the table of life. When we do that it is not humility at all; it's just humiliation, inaccurate self-esteem, and a destruction of a sound belief in our natural potential. As in the following story from the Iroquois, we can see just how powerful a cheerleader can be in preventing us from selling ourselves short because of past influences, cultural bias, or personal ignorance:

> The Iroquois Indians tell a fascinating story of a strange and unusual figure they call "the Peacemaker." The Peacemaker came to a village where the chief was known as "The Man-Who-Kills-and-Eats-People." Now the Man-Who-Kills-and-Eats-People, the chief, was in his wigwam. He had cut up his enemies and was cooking them in a massive pot in the center of the wigwam so that he might eat their flesh and absorb their mythical powers.

> The Peacemaker climbed to the top of the wigwam and looked down through the smokehole, say the Iroquois, and as he peered down through the smokehole his face was reflected in the grease on the top of the pot. And the Man-Who-Kills-and-Eats People looked into the pot, saw the reflection, and thought it to be his own face.

> And he said: "Look at that. That's not the face of a man who kills his enemies and eats them. Look at the

nobility. Look at the peace in that face. If that is my face, what am I doing carrying on this kind of a life?"

And he seized the pot, dragged it from the fire, brought it outside and poured it out on the ground. He then called the people and said: "I shall never again destroy or consume an enemy for I have discovered my true face. I have found out who I am."

And then, says the story, the Peacemaker came down from the top of the wigwam and embraced him and called him "Hiawatha."[24]

The third voice or type of friend necessary for the inner journey of humility is the teaser or *harasser*. This person is important to help us keep a sense of perspective about ourselves. In attempting to take life seriously we often take a detour and take ourselves too seriously instead. Helpers and healers are often guilty of this because of their intense work, but must learn not to lose a (sometimes wicked) sense of humor if they are to survive. Knowing this, the famous preacher Charles Haddon Spurgeon once said to a somber group of ministers: "You know, some ministers would make good martyrs. They are so dry they would burn well!" Truly humble people generally have a good sense of humor.

The final voice is that of the *wise companion* or *soul friend*. This is the individual in our life who calls us to be all that we can be without embarrassing us that we are where we are presently. Friends like this may never seem to say anything deeply spiritual or profoundly psychological.

But when we leave them we feel more integrated, whole, motivated, and centered. Soul friends are humble people who value life and, more specifically, our lives. This comes through clearly in their behavior and we are better able to understand and appreciate ourselves after our interactions with them. Such companions need not have an advanced academic degree or even a long life behind them to help us gain wisdom and a greater degree of humility. They help us honor ourselves and be grateful for the life we have. The following excerpt from a story by a professional counselor on her painful battle to correct a facial birth defect illustrates this quite poignantly.

> Through the years many companions have blessed me on my journey by imparting wisdom and lightening my load. My two-year-old niece was one of these surprising companions.
>
> I had just graduated from high school and was preparing to spend most of the next month in or near the hospital. I would be undergoing corrective facial surgery that was considered quite dangerous so naturally I was quite anxious about it.
>
> My niece, Shelly, had crawled into my suitcase because she wanted to go with me. She looked up and saw me crying as I was packing because I did not want to face what was ahead of me. When she saw this she looked straight into my eyes and said, "Don't cry. Jesus make it all better."

I was so caught up in my own preoccupations that I didn't pay much attention to this tiny angel's kind words. In a few hours, I left for the airport. Little did I realize that in a few short days, both of our lives would hang in the balance and be changed forever.

After the surgery, I experienced several serious complications. It was so bad that the staff prepared my family for the possibility that I might not make it through the night. While my sisters were on the phone together speaking and worrying about me, my niece Shelly unlatched the back door, went into the back yard, and fell into the swimming pool. Although she was gone but for a short while before her mother realized the silence in the house and her absence, it was long enough for her to have her little lungs fill with water, and drown.

Shelly died that night and I lived. I struggled with this for the longest time. I blamed myself and wallowed in self-pity. As Pema Chödrön says in her book *When Things Fall Apart*, we usually don't see pain as a source of potential wisdom. When something is painful we want to rid ourselves of the feeling as soon as possible and we even "cultivate a subtle aggression against ourselves." That description fit me exactly.

I wanted to rid myself of these feelings as soon as possible. I spent considerable time in prayer and meditation as well as in counseling, searching for a way to reconcile why I was here and she was gone. The person I least expected to die, died. The person I anticipated might die—me—survived. It was incon-ceivable to me. All my assumptions were challenged.

However, the experience eventually did give me a new perspective. As in the case of all people who are eventually able to surface from trauma, I let go of why it had to happen. Instead, the search for an answer eventually led me to a different place: the valuing of being in the present moment. There are no guaran-tees. All we have is this moment. There may not be a tomorrow. Those moments with Shelly were our last together on this earth. I realized I could take nothing for granted.

It's strange how we learn as children to believe life is fair. We make sure everyone has the same number of cookies. Everyone gets a ride on the pony. Then we grow up and discover, life is many things—but fair is not one of them.

I clung to Shelly's last words to me, "Jesus make it all better." I realized I had to trust God in this. If I did, I knew I could then choose to move out of the darkness and continue living my life—but in a different, more enlightened, way. I would take the lesson Shelly had taught me and move ahead as best as I could. I would also remember and take deeply to heart what one of my professors had taught me, "If we remain sensitive to the presence of God in faith and in prayer, and in the darkness of confusion and suffering, the darkness will teach us, it will become [new] light."[25]

The prophet, cheerleader, harasser, and wise companion are friends for the inner journey of humility. They complement our time in silence and solitude as well as help us to face those aspects of life that stand in opposition to a spirit of honesty, openness, and gratefulness. And, certainly among the obstacles to living humbly and simply that they guide us through, there is no greater one than a conscious sense of entitlement or the unconscious parallel danger of "repressed gratefulness."

BE GRATEFUL

Humility and a sense of entitlement are bad bed-fellows. If it is true that the meek shall inherit the earth, the entitled shall certainly contest their inheritance!

How did life become this way for so many of us? What happened to gratefulness, appreciation of the simple things in life, and a clear recognition that in the end *all* is gift? When did artificial needs become so powerfully consuming? Suggest to someone today that they can be happy with less and they think you are being absurd.

One of the difficulties may be that we can't seem to distinguish anymore between nice desires, fleeting fantasies, and what is essential for life. The line between wants and needs has become blurred. In the words of Abraham Heschel, "We usually fail to discern between authentic and artificial needs and, misjudging a whim for an aspiration, we are thrown into ugly tensions. Most obsessions are the perpetuation of such judgments. In fact, more people die in the epidemics of needs than in the epidemics of disease."[26] People obsessively chase what they don't need until they are overcome with resentment, undue stress, and anger that more often than not turns into violence. Even when aggression is not physical, a violent inner life is a sure way to develop psychosomatic disorders like headaches and ulcers as well as emotional and relational problems.

Ever since the so-called self-actualization movement of the 1960s, people have been taught that what they really must do to be truly happy is to step forward and get what is rightfully theirs. They must not stand back and be hesitant. They must be willing to take the necessary risks to get what they deserve out of life. I think this is the wrong risk for most people to take much of the time. To do so means that we spend most of our waking time constantly chasing and claiming rather than enjoying the life set before us. I believe that a more appropriate and powerful question that we should ask ourselves today is, "Am I taking enough risks to fully enjoy what I *already* have?"

Of course, this question is countercultural. It is tied more to a spirit of humility than a sense of entitlement. The consumer society we live in tries to keep us off balance. It urges us to be continuously in search of those things and people that are rightfully ours, and to believe that they will in the end, make us whole. It tries to convince us of three things. The first is to believe that we always should have *more*. The problem is that once we have more, it is never enough . . . we eventually want even more!

When this tactic doesn't work, the message is that to be happy we need something *different*. Yet, what is presently different soon becomes part of our norm. We quickly forget how wonderful any acquisition initially was. We soon forget how we had compulsively agonized over whether we should spend the money or make the effort to get it. Once convinced, gotten, and used for a while, it slips into a place where we forget it and maybe even tire of it. We have forgotten what it promised because in reality it doesn't deliver what we fantasized about and what society promised it would.

Finally, there is the elusive call to find the *perfect* (person, career, house, friend, "high") in life to make our inner selves happy. The only problem is, nothing like that exists in this world. Maybe the early Christian writer, Augustine of Hippo, was onto something when he indicated that our hearts would be restless until they rested in God. However, whether we believe this or not, we do know at some level that nothing will make our life totally painless or always filled with joy—no matter what we are told or promised.

Still there is no way to avoid the powerful and quite convincing call to buy, grasp, and own things which seem to promise so much in the future. We need to have a clear awareness and respect for the power of this reality in our culture today. We are being brainwashed into believing that living gratefully in freedom is an abstract fantasy. We are being told over and over again that owning more things, success, building up our image, or being liked by certain people or groups will make us happy, secure, comfortable, and strong—*in the future*. A bombardment of advertising has replaced a psychology and theology of hope with a spirit of greed and entitlement—even though somewhere in our hearts we know better.

John Berger in his book *Ways of Seeing* sheds light on one of the reasons this might be possible:

> Publicity speaks in the future tense and yet the achievement of this future is endlessly deferred. How then does publicity remain credible—or credible enough to exert the influence it does? It remains credible because truthfulness of publicity is judged, not by the real fulfillment of its promises, but by the relevance of its fantasies to those of the spectator-buyer. Its essential application is not to reality but to daydreams. No two dreams are the same. Some are instantaneous, others prolonged. The dream is always personal to the dreamer. Publicity does not manufacture the dream. All that it does is to propose to each one of us that we are not yet enviable—yet could be.[27]

The point I make here is that when—in a spirit of humility—we sit with a deep sense of gratefulness for all we are and have, we can enjoy life rather than postpone it.

Rather than grasping for something that will make things just right, we explore the many facets of our present life. This is a sound psychological approach. Healthy religion is wary of an unnecessarily extreme asceticism that always defers joy to some other time or even some other life. For instance, in the Jerusalem Talmud we read: "When you die God will hold you responsible for all of the gifts you have been given that you didn't enjoy." Whether we identify with a particular religious faith or not, a sure sign of psychological health is the desire to live our life fully. Otherwise we might miss, ignore, or belittle the wonderful people, personal gifts, and material possessions that are present to us. Humility gifts us with this. Humility fosters our knowledge of the truth about ourselves and the world around us. It allows us to be grateful and, in the process, not spend our entire lives in the paradoxical process of seeking more in the future while failing to enjoy what is already present. What a waste it is to do that. Yet, this is the conscious way of life for most of us. It is complicated even more by an unconscious problem that is rarely discussed called "repressed gratefulness."

Why Aren't We More Grateful?

When you ask people if they consider themselves to be grateful individuals, the invariable response is affirmative. Conscious ungratefulness is rare. The best response by some that we can expect is a sigh accompanying the comment, "Oh we have so much. We really should be more grateful." That is why many spiritual traditions include prayers of gratitude to remind people that it is a natural tendency to take things for granted.

From a psychological perspective, in my experience, truly grateful people are not just more honest and humble, they are also happier. They are convinced they have been and are currently being gifted in so many ways. As a result, they look back on their lives in a way that acknowledges these gifts. This gives them a sense of fulfillment rather than regret. They also look at their lives in the present and see what is good so they can enjoy it and look to the future with positive expectations. Usually this prophecy is fulfilled because they are able to see the good even when faced with the pain we all must experience at certain stages of our lives.

One of my students was a living example of this for me. In her final paper, she illustrated it:

> It was the day after Christmas, 1995. My mother and I were on the phone working out logistics for when we would meet at my grandmother's. We had spent Christmas day with my father's relatives so this would balance out our seasonal visits. We were really looking forward to it since I truly loved my Nana, as we affectionately called her.
>
> During our conversation, my mother who has call waiting on her telephone, received a beep telling her another caller was on the line. After putting me on hold and getting it, she was quickly back on the line.

Breathlessly she said, "Meet me at shock trauma at St. Agnes Hospital. Nana has been in an accident and they are taking her there."

This must be really bad for them to take her to shock trauma. But she's alive and she's strong, I thought as I rushed to the hospital.

Nana had experienced a serious head injury. The doctor told us if she lived, she would be incapacitated for the rest of her life. After hearing this, the "if onlys" set in. If only I had seen her on Christmas. If only the person whose car struck her down had not been distraught about losing his job. If only. . . .

The days turned into weeks and then months. Nana was finally moved from shock trauma. For the next nine months she would go back and forth from the hospital to nursing homes. She was never able to speak again but sometimes I would look into her eyes and she would communicate to me by crying. I would sometimes wonder if deep within she was alert yet trapped in a body no longer able to function.

I had been thinking that I wanted to have an intimate worship experience with my Nana. I would pray and read the Bible and sing praises like she used to sing to me when I was a little girl. Just me and Nana worshipping together. Yes that's what I wanted.

It seems as though God worked things out for us, but with an added surprise or two. For some reason on one particular Sunday, Nana didn't have any other visitors so I saw my chance. I closed the curtain between the patient in the next bed and Nana and what a joyous time was had with the Lord! Then, after several songs, the other elderly patient in the next bed cried out, "Sing to me too!" I pushed back the curtain and the three of us—and God—communed together. What a lively worship service we had!

The next morning my mother called me to tell me that Nana had passed away in the middle of the night. When I heard that, I couldn't help but thank God for His compassion for allowing me to have such a special fellowship on the eve of her going home. I thought then of the way one of my teacher's perspectives about a healthy way to face the difficulties we must all encounter in life: "Concern doesn't deny there is a problem. It faces the issues directly. However, it then musters the thought, 'How can I sit with this trouble in a good way?'"

In reading a story like this, many questions arise: Why aren't most of us like this more of the time? Why is it that we are not grateful in the good times but rather take them for granted? Why is it that when we are faced with the inevitable pains that must come in every life, that we are not looking through grateful eyes at some point to see what good we can glean from it? Or, from the standpoint of our interactions with others, Why is it that we tend to gloss over positive feedback and take negative feedback so seriously?

Of course there are many answers to these questions. However, when we speak of an intractable unconscious lack of gratitude, I think one of the main reasons is fear. There is a deep fear that one will not get enough out of life in certain ways to be happy. This usually starts quietly—preverbally and nonverbally—when we are very young. Some world cultures even seem to teach it to their children and thrive on it and manifest an almost radical resistance to expressing thanks for anything. The attitude is based on an interesting philosophy or theology: If God (or my neighbors) see that I have a lot to be grateful for, then surely they will be jealous, it will be taken away or I will never get more in life.

People suffering from a style of living marked by ungratefulness miss seeing it in their own personality. As a result, both they, and the persons around them, suffer. Even when they do say thank you, their gratitude is tainted. They say it because others expect it, politically it's the right thing to do, or they like the person they are thanking and want to be appreciated in return for being seen as a grateful person. This is pretty sad when you think about it. Yet, little, if any, of this is done consciously, so blaming them for it or expecting them to change should you point it out is a waste of time. Worse, it leads to resentment on our part, is upsetting for us, and may lead to the unconscious seeking of revenge against the person suffering from this hidden problem. I remember making this same mistake in my own life in how I treated a colleague. He was someone who could certainly have been diagnosed as an unintentional martyr, or as my mother would say, "a poor sock." Luckily I had a couple of trusted friends who guided me to the point where I could see my immature motives.

Shortly after graduation from my doctoral studies, there was another colleague who was extremely talented and industrious. Amazingly though, he also suffered from an unrecognized (both on his part and mine) serious case of repressed gratefulness. Everyone around him seemed to see that he felt unappreciated. He would demonstrate it in an off-handed remark, derisive laugh, or half-hearted appreciation of compliments. If a colleague was recognized or the staff received a gift, he would comment about it— always with a short laugh. Often he would say something that would point out that they were always appreciated and people like him weren't. When he was given recognition by the chairperson of the department via an e-mail or letter, this didn't seem to satisfy him either. He had a fascinating way of deflating compliments: "I got your card and know you probably sent similar notes to a number of the faculty but I am grateful not to be left out."

I decided (with unconscious grandiosity) that I would take him on as a "kindness project." I believed that if he were shown how wonderful he was, he would finally stop appearing so needy. This would then lead to others finding him more interpersonally attractive and would, in the end, add further joy to his life. To accomplish this I did all I could to show him how talented and wonderful he was.

I also did my best to see that he was unburdened of any unnecessary work and given credit for the high level of performance he achieved in what he was assigned. (Don't forget he actually was someone who was extremely talented and appreciated when he didn't come across to others as arrogant or ungrateful.) Unfortunately, in the end, I became discouraged and gave up. Also, my imperfect motivation for helping him wound up causing suffering for both of us because my actions were not really given as an unattached gift. Instead, without my really realizing it, I wanted him to change for *my* sake. I wanted him to be grateful to *me*.

Even though it is over twenty years since this happened, he still includes me among the people on whom he couldn't count and remains convinced that he is unappreciated, misused, and set aside. Paradoxically, I do believe that even now if he really were able to take a step back in quiet reflection and receive the support and challenge of persons less grandiose and more psychologically healthy than I was at the time, he would see the world differently than he does now and be free. It would break the negative cycle and he would have a much happier life. But, if this cycle goes unbroken, I am afraid he will remain sad, feel unappreciated, rejected, and be an unnecessary martyr. It takes a good deal of courage to let go of habitual destructive ways of viewing the world and our inner selves. Unfortunately, the very views that hold us back are the ones that appear to us as "friends" that only have the best intentions for us. There is a lot of wisdom in the old say-ing: The truth shall set you free . . . but first it will make you miserable!

A true spirit of humility helps us to see our gifts and growing edges with a sense of equanimity. True humility helps us let go of our sense of entitlement, rejoice, and be grateful for all material and personal gifts we have been given in life—especially the gift of who we are. To have such an experience is not narcissism or pride. It's a sense of pure joy to recognize that we've been given intelligence, a sunrise to see, a good disposition, friends at different points in life, or whatever or whomever we have in our lives for which to be thankful. True humility allows us to enjoy and lift the bushel basket off our talents for everyone in the world to see. We are able to do this without falling into the trap of being an egomaniac because when we are truly honest about our gifts we also can simultane-ously see our "sins" or defensive areas. Our lives become transparent.

In most world spiritualities, there is a wonderful recog-nition of how we can and should constantly embrace true humility by seeing ourselves directly without a coating of psychological makeup. In essence, it states that we must constantly look at those areas in which we are unfree, sin-ful, or defensive—however one's tradition or approach casts it. Simultaneously, we must never forget to see and be truly pleased that we are gifted by what is referred to in some Christian theology as being made in the image and likeness of God ("*imago Dei*"), a loving person capable of true compassion.

After a session of sitting *zazen* (quiet group meditation) with his disciples, Zen Master Shunryu Suzuki put humility's paradoxical quality of being grateful, yet totally honest, about who we are, to them this way. He said, "You are all perfect as you are." Then, after a short pause, with, I suspect, a twinkle in his eye, he quickly added, "But you could all use a little improvement."[28]

Deep gratefulness and humility go hand in hand because the issue of quantity—something valued in a consumer society—falls by the wayside. Instead, with a spirit of "all is gift," so much more around and in us is appreciated. That gift might seem insignificant without the humility and gratefulness to open our eyes and ears to all that we are given each day.

The senior *dharma* teacher Norman Fischer puts this beautifully in the following experience that he was able to embrace because of the humility and gratefulness he was experiencing in that moment: "Last night I went to sleep. I heard an owl. At that moment I truly didn't need or want anything else for my life, nor did I have the thought that I did not need nor want anything. Just 'hoot, hoot.'"[29]

How often all of us have had small but meaningful experiences such as this and let them slip by. Maybe we have sat inside a warm house wrapped in a oversized, cuddly sweater on a bitter day, had a stirring and encouraging conversation with a dear friend, eaten a crisp salad that crunched with each bite, or laughed and had our thoughts twinkle as we read a poem, but still didn't fully recognize these moments for what they were: epiphanies of wonder and awe for which to be grateful.

Sadly, more often than not, we don't see the daily joys of life in this way. Like society in general, negative feelings or a sense of distance from our inner selves are our natural, spontaneous responses to life. Contrary to this, a spirit of humble gratitude slows us down to recognize the need to pace our life differently so we can see ourselves, life, and our surroundings in a new way. Sometimes, as in the following reflection shared with me by a former student about her father, we can appreciate this in the amazing people who treasure and live out a gift marked by a simple strong faith. It is then that their strength and sense of life-giving perspective may become an anchor or beacon for us—whether we believe exactly in what they do or not. With the right attitude or perspective we can let go and see that new possibilities can arise in the human psyche no matter how dark things become.

> My father was diagnosed with pancreatic cancer and suffered for four months until his death. During these months I began to question God about how my father had to die. If it had to happen now, why did it have to be so painful? He was slowly slipping away and suffering as he did. Couldn't it just end quickly for someone who was so faithful to the Lord?

My father trusted the Lord and accepted His will. He had accepted the diagnosis and encouraged us to discuss his illness and death. So, then, I spoke to my father about this struggle I was having with God. My father saw the situation very differently than I did. He believed God was being faithful and keeping a promise. He saw this time as a gift. Even in the suffering, he was grateful. He was able to wrap up his affairs, say his good-byes, impart wisdom and surround himself with those he loved. He was able to spend the last weeks of his life preparing to be with his God. Since this was the way he had lived his life, this is the way he wanted to die. Since his family meant so much to him, he would not have been happy leaving us suddenly. Instead, he was allowed to minister until the end. I was so preoccupied with the way I thought the end should be for my father that I did not realize that this could be an answer to prayer.

After this conversation with my father, I became more sensitive to what was happening around me. My counseling relationship at that time also brought clarity. Once I let go of my preoccupations, I was able to be fully present to my father in the moment. This also allowed me to be open to new insight and understanding.

I was struck by my father's gratitude. He seemed grateful for the smallest of things. He appreciated every moment and all of God's gifts. For example, he managed to enjoy food even though he could no longer digest it properly and was limited to liquids.

I remember sitting by his bedside feeding him roast beef. He put a piece in his mouth and rolled it around. His eyes closed and he had a look of sheer pleasure on his face. Unfortunately, he could not swallow this food or he would become very ill. Digesting the food mattered little to him. He could still taste it and that was more than enough. When I think of all the meals I did not fully appreciate because I was in a hurry, it makes me realize how ungrateful I can be. At the end of his life, my father was teaching me about gratitude, faithfulness and being open to God's mercy. Now when I reflect at the end of each day, I find myself asking the question my father always posed, "What do you thank your God for today?"

We may never be as amazingly grateful and humble as this man or have his ability to find the best sense of perspective possible when faced with the tough realities of life. Yet, maybe like his wonderfully open daughter, we also can learn to move more in that direction. Certainly, the interaction of humility and gratefulness represents a core curriculum in and of itself, filled with psychological and spiritual lessons, on how to seek such a healthy attitude from this very moment of our lives until its final end.

But, in a spirit of humility, to do this, we must be willing to let go and give up the security of thinking we know more than we do. We must be willing to constantly sit on the edge of mystery and *un*learn what has helped guide us in the past but is no longer as useful now. To do this we must be willing to ask the questions that will open us up to hear the quiet, powerful voice of freedom. In other words, we must be willing to ask the four classic questions of the desert designed to help us let go of old ways of seeing life so we can experience the true freedom for which we know we truly yearn.

part two

LETTING GO

six

ASK THE FOUR DESERT
QUESTIONS

The desert *ammas* and *abbas* of the fourth century
saw that worry, tensions, pride, greed, fear, and
a desire for power and fame filled much of the
world, and even the church. This led them to embrace a
spirit of letting go. It moved them to ask some form of the
question: What am I filled with now that is holding me
back? This is the most basic question all of us must deal
with on the journey toward letting go of all that is unnecessary and destructive in ourselves.

THE FIRST QUESTION: *What Am I Filled with Now?*

One of the lessons we all must learn if we are to survive spiritually and psychologically is how to leave behind what is unnecessary and travel light. Alan Jones relates a story whose imagery brings this across quite well.

> It is said that during an uprising in India late in the last century when British service families had to be evacuated, the road was strewn with such things as stuffed owls and Victorian bric-a-brac. I have no idea what the late twentieth century equivalent of a stuffed owl is, but no doubt our path will be just as littered with such "necessities." We will have to learn to travel light.[30]

What we carry and *why* we carry it are two areas that must be examined from both a psychological and spiritual perspective. The why is connected with *trusting* enough in God to open ourselves up to seeing clearly. The what refers to looking at our perceived needs in order to see if they are real needs or idols that trap us. According to Rabbi Abraham Joshua Heschel,

> Needs are looked upon today as if they were holy, as if they contained the quintessence of eternity. Needs are our gods, and we toil and spare no effort to gratify them. Suppression of desire is considered a sacrilege that must inevitably avenge itself in the form of some mental disorder. . . . We feel jailed in the confinement of personal needs. The more we indulge in satisfactions, the deeper is our feeling of oppressiveness. . . .

> We must be able to say *no* to ourselves in the name of a higher *yes*.[31]

While initially this "no" may cause us pain and confusion, it will be possible if we are able to see the freedom that results from it as a "pearl of great price," as something that is worth giving everything up for. To do this, the *ammas* and *abbas* looked at both trust in God and at the needs that were imprisoning people.

In the desert, the Fathers and Mothers of the fourth century were aware that trust in God had to be nurtured. But even when they were confronted with the marvelous graciousness of God, it did not always lead to greater trust and freedom. In the fourth century as now—though we may not recognize it in the midst of abundance—we often see life and its challenges through non-trusting eyes. Like the monk in this story, we may have also witnessed a miracle but had to be given the even greater grace of awareness of our deep lack of trust.

> One day, when Abba Bessarion and I were walking along the sea I became very thirsty and shared this. In response, the elder prayed and then told me to drink from the sea. I did and the water was sweet. After I finished I poured some into a flask so I would not be thirsty later on in the day. Seeing this, the old man asked me, "Why are you doing that?" I responded, "Pardon me Father, it is so I won't be thirsty later on." To which he responded simply, "God is here; God is *everywhere*."[32]

Reliance on God in our lives may be much more theoretical in nature than we realize. Perhaps this is because we have taken care of many of our own needs—or at least we think we have. God then becomes superfluous to us without our knowing it until those times come—and they always will—when we can find no solace in our own abilities or usual supports. Then a true realization that everything comes from God results in a sense of awe, maybe even fear of the Lord. The Desert Fathers and Mothers and their apprentices tried to counter this tendency toward self-reliance by developing a sense of compunction and an attitude that was based on a need for God at all times. Yet, even in the desert this was difficult because of the natural human tendency to protect oneself.

This situation once prompted a senior brother to ask the respected Abba Poemen how he could gain a helpful fear of the Lord so as not to forget his ultimate reliance on the gifts of God. To which the elder responded: "How indeed? Especially since our stomachs are full of cheese and our cells [rooms] filled with jars of salted fish."[33]

Being filled, though, is not just having things or physical possessions that we want. On a deeper level, it is also a sense of being filled with our own ego, self-interest, desires, and self-righteousness. This prompted one of the Desert Fathers to say, "I prefer a sinner if he admits it and repents over someone who says he has not sinned and therefore considers himself righteous." In line with this, another Father, Abba Poemen said, "There is one type of person who appears to be silent. Yet, inwardly he is constantly criticizing others. Whereas, there is another person who may talk from morning until night, but says only what is essential, and so actually keeps silence."[34] And so, the first question is, "Where am I unfree (full, attached, caught, addicted, blind) now?"

Recognizing that there is always some aspect of our lives where we are caught is an important first step toward loosening the grasp of that which binds us. It is sometimes a very difficult step to take. Harriet Tubman, for example, when congratulated for freeing so many slaves during the Civil War, didn't respond with joy. Instead, she sadly replied, "Actually I could have freed thousands more . . . only they didn't know they were slaves." Are we humble enough to open the door to seeing those areas in which we are slaves, or is this bondage so much a part of us that we aren't willing or even able to recognize it anymore?

There is a Chinese proverb: "He has too many tics to feel the itch." Most of us, if we are honest, will admit that we don't know we are "full" or trapped in some way. This is a shame because with just a little humility, intrigue, and a few questions, we can be released from what has caught us. When we recognize that we are indeed caught, the results need not simply be guilt or shame. Instead it can be the freedom that such a true awareness or insight brings with it.

Joseph Goldstein, a Zen Master, was once very upset about an interaction he had with a person that he thought to be his friend. He felt stabbed in the back by this person. Then, during a period of sitting *zazen* he achieved a realization that freed him. In relating it to others he said, "I realized for the knife to hurt it needed some place to land. This focused my attention so I could do something." With this awareness, he could then ask, "Where was *I* getting caught?"[35]

Recognizing the signs of a lack of freedom helps us to embrace this first question. To do this we have to begin to look at ourselves with a sense of intrigue rather than projecting the blame outward, being harsh toward ourselves, or looking for the easy way out of the many situations we do not like. Just as in the fourth-century desert and in the case of contemporary Zen Master Joseph Goldstein just cited, we must question ourselves in ways that allow new knowledge to rise to the surface. For example, when we are intrigued by our feelings, thoughts, perceptions, ways of understanding and behavior, some of the questions that will prove helpful include the following.

Where do we spend the most time, energy, emotion, preoccupation, judgment, blame, and resentment? This will help us diagnose where we are stuck and see what idol or god is taking most of our energy and concern.

What in our life represents what I like to refer to as "the myth of the one flower"? By this I mean: What in our life do we believe is absolutely essential for our happiness? Or, what do we believe must happen for our life to be perfect? They may be good things to wish for, appreciate, or want, but the question still remains: Why have we turned them into gods that have caused us to forfeit all our happiness, joy, and peace—especially since there is the reality of *impermanence,* and all things shall pass?

When do we become moody? This is a sign that we are filled with the wrong things and have become over-involved in ourselves; we need the perspective that compassion and reaching out beyond our small world brings with it.

In our choices and decisions, what are all *our motivations?* Our intentions are never pure. There are always reasons that are less than mature. *Everyone* should question his or her own integrity. As a matter of fact, paradoxically, it is one of the best ways to have greater integrity. If or when our motivations are called into question we need to be open so we can experience the gifts that come with a stance of welcoming new knowledge.

What are our automatic negative interpretations and responses? In many cases, our first reaction to a new or unexpected situation is to get angry, become afraid, be sad or resentful, even to experience despair. Even little things, such as being cut off by another driver on the highway, may lead to dramatic negative responses. Such a habitual unpleasant response means we are filled with the wrong things.

The fruits of freedom and emptiness ripen when we face these questions. They include less desire, less unprocessed anger, and less hatred. When we are not so caught by things in life, there is a greater sense of calm, less of a tendency to take everything so seriously, a decrease in judgmental attitudes, a better sense of simplicity. There is also an increased ability, when it is psychologically or spiritually dark, to separate the clouds of life so we can be discerning and see the sky behind them. Perspective, flowing rather than drifting with life, and a having a greater sense of peace are all fruits of being empty.

Yet, even when we try to be honest with ourselves, we may still have difficulty in facing ourselves and letting go. There is a second question that must also come up again and again at each stage of life, especially during our desert experiences of loss, pain, dramatic change, and inner darkness. It looks at what is blocking purity of heart, transparency, and awareness. There must be a logic to our staying imprisoned, but what is it?

The Second Question: *What Prevents Me from Letting Go?*

Realizing that we are not free, open, or detached is the essential first step. Your interest in desert wisdom is a wonderful affirmation that you are already embracing this question to some degree. The next challenge is to uncover hidden resistances to letting go of the very things that are holding you back and harming you—even though they may appear to be protecting vulnerable parts of your life in some way. Sometimes these things are obvious if you look.

Knowing what to let go of and when to let go is an undervalued art, rarely practiced. We sometimes hold onto things that are hurting us deeply, perhaps because we don't know that any other course of action is possible. Or, we wonder if it is worth the trouble to change. Familiarity, habit, and the fear of change all imprison us.

To some extent, each of us is caught like this in some area of our lives. No matter how intelligent, gifted, mature, or accomplished we are, letting go is still an elusive step for most of us. As a matter of fact, we may often be free and flowing in one area but caught in another. The two states can exist side by side.

I know someone who has dazzled me for over ten years with his talents as a speaker. Not only does he deliver his message well, but his development of a theme shows a broad grasp of both classic literature and the challenges of modern life. After listening to one of his talks I feel an amazing sense of insight and am personally challenged to live more deeply and authentically. He encourages me to let down my defenses and let go of my inordinate self-interest so I can be present to others in a more transparent way. His message is: Be free for yourself so you can be transparent and generous to others. He is amazingly gifted in this way.

However, in his role as C.E.O. of a large nonprofit institution, he seems to be wearing blinders. He is not open to the possibility of leaving his post for a new calling—maybe to something even greater. He becomes very angry if someone tries to remove the blinders to enable him to see that while he has contributed much in the past, it is now time for him to let go in this area of his life.

Yet, my judgment of him is tempered by a dim awareness of the blinders that I too wear, the blocks I have put in my own life. How often have I held on in both small and large ways long after there was ample evidence from others that I should let go and move on in some area of my life. Often it was only after I had bouts of prolonged anger or feelings of being misunderstood that I sensed these emotions were telling me more about my *own* sense of fear of change than they were about standing up for myself. It seems we hold on tightest to the very things or people that prevent us from being truly free. Without knowing it, we are prevented from developing a healthy sense of detachment.

In his book *Experiencing God,* Kenneth Leech describes how religion can be used as a crutch blocking us from the inner freedom to take responsibility for our own choices in life. In the language of the desert, he describes it this way:

> [D]etachment from dependence on created things and other people and false ideas of self can often seem dangerously close to atheism, for faith rejects false piety. To enter the desert is to leave behind the trappings of religion in so far as these keep us from facing reality. And that separation can be very painful for

the trappings will be associated with people, whose friendship and support we have come to value, but who without knowing it are helping to preserve us in immaturity and prevent our progress. The path into the desert is a lonely path, requiring courage and the willingness to trust the obscurity and uncertainty of the road—and the obscure God who calls us forward . . . detachment is seen in negative terms as long as we see the process from the human side. If we are able to see it from the perspective of God, it might be possible to see the process as a clothing, a process of divinization, of the taking of our humanity into God.[36]

So, what are some of the main reasons why we don't let go? Why do we keep doing the same negative things over and over, maybe even more efficiently? The spiritual teacher Anthony de Mello described this pattern as a self-made prison. We may not know we are in prison, we may put curtains on the prison bars, we may even organize a prison reform group. We may think of these as ways out of the prison. Instead, he said, what we must do is be aware of our prison bars, realize we are responsible for locking ourselves in, and simply unlock our psychological and spiritual doors and walk out! Walking out of our prisons seems simple, but it does require some caution and awareness of certain wrong directions we can take. Among such errors are the following attitudes and tendencies.

We may tend to either shrug off blame or cling to it rather than simply being intrigued by what is going on in us. The two errors in this area are *projection of blame* onto others, which leads to our giving all the power for improvement to others, and *being harsh with ourselves,* which only leads to self-hatred. Instead, we can respond by giving feedback to ourselves (or to others in those times when we are called to be a mentor). But we must do so without punishment. There are a number of reasons why the Desert Fathers and Mothers could do this. They embraced sacred scripture and thus realized the role of grace and the place of God. They knew that falling short or sinning was natural. They also knew that they needed the word of God, and periods of silence and solitude so they could reassess their lives. They knew that they needed feedback from others and appreciated at a deep level that to try to do it on their own was pure folly.

Discouragement also makes us pull back from seeking purity of heart. Hesitancy about seeking clarity about ourselves and our mission in life is just as present today as it was in the fourth century. The movement from *chronos,* ordinary time, to *kairos,* the time in which God breaks through, helps us appreciate that God's time is not our time. It allows for patience and a recognition that the struggle to see life clearly and let go of what is harming us is a life-long journey. As Thomas Merton would advise in modern times, it is natural to feel the pain of our constant mistakes. But why should we feel desperation? That is unnecessary, especially when we recognize that God is always present and that grace flows in our lives. This is the sense of time that the Desert Fathers and Mothers had.

Anger, hurt, fear, and lack of trust also keep us from seeing the truth. These attitudes can lead us to replace the living God with an image or set of doctrines that we can control. There is an unconscious desire to rest *not* in God but in dogma and set beliefs so we don't have to take responsibility for ourselves. The Dalai Lama was asked by a well-known *rinpoche* (precious teacher) just after the Chinese invaded Tibet, what he should do—stay or leave? The Dalai Lama responded, "Well now brother everyone stands on his own two feet." Thomas Merton, who had met the Dalai Lama, later interpreted this statement in terms of the spiritual life. He affirmed that everyone, at some point, has to have the courage to stand on his own faith. In our inner deserts of darkness and impasse, this is exactly what we are being called to do—to leap into the darkness of God to find the truth that will teach us new ways to love and be free.

A lack of humility also prevents us from letting go of our views or discovering how petty and selfish we can be. If asked whether we are generous, most of us would say, "Why, yes." It is very hard to be aware of our own insensitivity and unhealthy self-interest. It is almost unnatural. In the deserts of our lives, the goal is to uncover our different levels of insensitivity. This is not to punish ourselves, but to free us from those very elements that come disguised as friends (i.e., concerns about whether we have *enough*, are protected *enough*, are respected *enough*). But when is enough, enough? To ask this question and others like it takes humility. This same humility was in fact at the heart of the fourth-century pursuit of purity of heart.

Self-blame can also keep us from letting go. When resistance to change is conscious on our part, we wind up blaming ourselves rather than seeking to understand ourselves. We need to recognize that knowing when and how we block ourselves is in itself very helpful for us. And so, we should really view resistance in this way, not merely as something to be conquered or pointed to as evidence that we are shameful people. Nothing is usually accomplished when such views come into play.

This last point is worth expanding upon a bit. Knowing the current psychological perspective about resistance may help us be more aware of our shortcomings. This is important so we don't fall prey to self-condemnation when we seem to make the same mistakes again and again.

At one time, when the science of psychology was still young, a client who resisted change was thought to lack *motivation*. If someone did not make the change the counselor proposed, there was a sense that the counselor had done his or her job and it was the client's fault for not embracing the change. The only thing more that the counselor could do was to try to help the client identify the resistance to change and motivate the person to try again.

Today psychologists recognize that resistance to change is not simply a motivational problem. The client is not deliberately giving people a hard time. Rather, the resistance to change is seen as a source of critical information about the problematic areas of the client's life. This information can become a real source of understanding for psychological growth and spiritual insight.

While motivation is essential for growth, psychologists recognize that knowledge about oneself is equal in importance to the desire to actively make change. In a nutshell: *Motivation or positive thinking is good, but it is obviously not enough.*[37]

What is clear then is that we also need to know how to deal with this resistance to emptying ourselves of all that is unnecessary and harmful to us. The Desert Fathers and Mothers knew all about resistance and have taught us much. In addition, clinical psychology today has much to teach. The following summary of ways to approach our resistances indirectly and to deal with them in a productive way is an example; it certainly is in line with sound spirituality and can be a tool for what we wish to accomplish in seeking to let go and be free.

Increasing Sensitivity to Resistances to Change . . . and Outflanking Them

When we seek to export the blame for problems in our life, psychologists call it projection. This defensive style is manifested in ways that may be both obvious and quiet. They include denying our role in mistakes or failures, excusing our behavior, contextualizing our actions, absolving ourselves, rationalizing failures, and generally removing ourselves from the equation while focusing on the negative roles others have played.

Part of the reason we do this is that when we try to take responsibility for our own role in various unpalatable events, we go overboard. Instead of trying to understand what part we played so we can learn from it, we move from remorse about what we've done to shame about who we are. We can tell when this occurs because we start to condemn ourselves, become hypercritical of our behavior, unrealistic in our comparison with others in the field, and overly responsible with respect to the impact we did and can have. We become perfectionists.

Instead, we need to take a step back from the event and try to frame the situation in an objective way. We should behave as if it were someone else we were looking at and seek to become intrigued about our behavior. This helps to avoid overly blaming others, condemning oneself, or getting discouraged when results don't happen immediately. To further reduce the resistance to change, several caveats can help us outflank the blocks to growth:

1. Anything discovered does not have to be changed immediately;
2. No area should be condemned . . . just neutrally observed as if it were happening to someone else;

3. No area should be defended—no one is criticizing or attacking, just observing where the energy is being spent;

4. Observations—even disturbing ones—should be embraced as a wonderful treasure trove of information;

5. After each period of observation, the areas of concern should be written down so some record is kept of discovery.

Classic signs that we are holding on include:

- arguing,

- not sharing all the information or motivations with persons with whom we discuss the event,

- complaining that change in certain areas is unrealistic,

- stonewalling persons through an icy silence or monopolizing the situation,

- feeling misunderstood or totally ignored,

- other strong emotions or off-putting actions.

On the other hand, there are also classic signs that a person does value change, growth, and insight both professionally and personally. Some of these signs are:

- an ability to let go;

- receptive to new lessons;

- not self-righteous;

- intrigue with one's own emotional flashing lights;
- disgust with . . . the endless wheel of suffering that comes from grasping and bad habits;
- curious, not judgmental;
- values experience;
- recognizes danger of preferences which prevent experiencing new gifts in life;
- being awake to present and is mindful;
- appreciates quiet meditation;
- generous and alive;
- learns, reflects, and applies wisdom to daily life; and
- rests lightly in life.[38]

Taking both classic spirituality and the modern psychology that supports it into account gives us a richer understanding of resistance as a source of new knowledge rather than simply a hurdle to be leaped over. When we view it this way, then emptiness, transparency, or purity of heart becomes a continual goal that is part of life. Seeking freedom is not frustrating in this light but a constant process of exploration. Although it is not always a straight path, it is always supported, in both darkness and light, by God's love and call to let go.

THE THIRD QUESTION: *How Do I Empty Myself?*

As we have seen, the process of letting go requires us to recognize that we are not free and appreciate that resistance to change is both a part of the human condition and a treasure trove of information on where and why we are holding on. The next natural challenge we must face is to recognize what preoccupies or worries us unnecessarily. Or, more broadly, to ask (in terms Zen Buddhists would also embrace), "How do we empty ourselves?" This question is directly addressed by many of the sayings of the Desert Fathers and Mothers. Their responses to this question often emphasized the need for silence and solitude. These set the stage for greater clarity and the freedom to love God and neighbor, the natural fruits of such purity of heart.

As is typical of the sayings, the form such advice took was often quite simple. For instance, when a young brother approached Abba Moses for some simple advice on how to develop a healthy and strong spiritual life, he might have expected some Herculean task. Instead, the old man simply replied, "Go into your room alone and your room will teach you everything." Later on, another Desert Father echoed this theme with a slightly different emphasis: "Constant prayer will quickly clear up your confusion."

For us today, a little time each morning in quiet contemplation seeds a centered day marked by greater perspective and a sense of openness. Taking a few breaths during the day to reflect back on this period renews and reorients us when elusive perspective is once again lost. It is a circle of grace: quiet morning prayer leads into daily prayerfulness; prayerfulness sets the stage for a future period of intentional contemplation at day's end.

Because they are so rare, silence and solitude provide us with surprises that can open us up. There is a sense today, a myth really, that silence exists at the root of everything, and noise is something added. In contemporary society this is far from true. In Daniel Mason's novel *The Piano Tuner* the main character doesn't realize that he has gotten so used to the sound of the ship he is traveling on until there is a change: "The following morning, Edgar was awakened by the sudden arrival of silence. The steamboat, after groaning relentlessly for seven days, cut her engines and drifted. New sounds [then] slipped into the cabin."[39]

This episode is a good metaphor for what happens when we settle down in silence and, if possible, solitude, to contemplate. Silence awakens us to the sounds that are just below our level of awareness (the preconscious) by creating a space in our consciousness. When we quiet down, these sounds and mental gossip slip into our level of awareness. This information can be very helpful in the process of self-awareness and letting go, but we often don't greet such revelations in this way. If we are honest with ourselves we must admit that we are often upset by what we perceive as unpleasant thoughts about ourselves. In this way, we are just like the desert dwellers of the fourth century who were often confused and discouraged by their image-shattering thoughts, ego-games, and shame when they came to light during quiet periods of solitude. So, we are in good company!

Our image is very precious to us, and even in the fourth century it was obvious to the desert elders that this was both a temptation and a danger. Abba Silvanius once said, "Woe to the person whose fame is greater than his achievements." The desire to build ourselves up in our own eyes and the eyes of others is a natural wish. The desire to avoid, deny, minimize, rationalize, or excuse our behavior or impulses is also natural. Likewise, being oversensitive to our own faults is an age-old problem as well.

This should not be surprising. With any effort to seek the good, our initial steps can be quite difficult. The Desert Fathers and Mothers were aware of this. To deal with it, they also shared and modeled for apprentices the great joy, peace, and freedom that comes from silence and solitude as well as the helpful information that surfaces when we are faithful in prayer.

Once this process begins we also need to appreciate that there is no "spiritual graduation." Accomplishment is not the goal, *faithfulness* is. For instance, it was said of the respected Abba Pior that "each day of his life he made a fresh beginning." Every day the goal is to increase our wisdom and be more natural and free in our compassion. When we try to be wiser and it doesn't work, then we should at least try not to regress. If we seek to be compassionate and find we are grumpy and ungrateful on a particular day, then we should at least have the decency to keep our mouths shut and try not to be a pest to others. The quest in itself (freedom) is not a destination where one can finally rest on one's laurels or abilities. It is a constant endeavor of being intrigued by one's inner life and seeking to be present to it in a way that seeks meaning and good energy. From a Christian perspective, German theologian Rudolf Bultmann reminds us, "Grace can never be possessed. It must be received afresh again and again."

A helpful caution and note of guidance in this regard is contained in the following three suggestions passed down from desert disciple to desert disciple through the years:

1. Do not be proud of your spiritual accomplishments;
2. Don't worry excessively once you have made an effort to do what is right;
3. Curb your desires and tendency to gossip about others.

Due to the state of society today with its emphasis on greed, security, fame, staying young, denying death, self-interest, and competitiveness, this is a tall order. We must recognize that much of our journey will be countercultural. One respected Desert Father foresaw this seventeen centuries ago and said, "The time will soon be here when most people will be insane, and when they see someone who is not, they will reject that person because he is different from them." That is why there is no stopping after the third question; one must move to the fourth and final one or risk worse problems. As Jesus warned us: once the room is swept clean there is clearly a danger that worse demons will fill it down the road.

"Spiritual dieting" to empty ourselves of the crippling defenses and unhealthy ego activities that fill us is not enough. Just as studies of physical dieting statistics demonstrate, after they reach their weight goal most people not only eventually gain the weight back but add that and more! So, in desert spiritual wisdom, the emptiness beckons us to face a truly mysterious question about our next step on the pilgrimage toward freedom and purity of heart at this stage of our life.

THE FOURTH QUESTION: *What Will Satisfy Me Yet Leave Me Open to More?*

Among the many additional ways we could express this fourth question are the following:

- Once I am empty, what do I fill myself with?

- What do I do once the room is swept clean?

- What will give me new life, a deeper sense of freedom, and a single-heartedness that is countercultural to the fragmented world around me?

- In essence, what paradoxically will satisfy me but still leave me spiritually open, empty, and free?

Anyone we may identify as a role model has undoubtedly faced this question in some form, whether in a single dramatic encounter or as a series of events. One good example is the former Archbishop of Chicago, Cardinal Joseph Bernadin. He faced a serious charge by a young man, a church in crisis that he sought to mend, and eventually the onset of a terminal illness. The story of his constant healing presence to others through it all began behind the scenes long before these events happened. It is related in the following sensitive way by Robert Ellsberg in his encouraging work, *The Saints Guide to Happiness*:

> The story [of Cardinal Bernadin's final road to spiritual growth and compassion] began some years before, when a group of fellow priests confronted him with a challenging question. They asked him to consider whether his life was focused more on the church or on Christ. Their question had a profound impact, causing Bernadin to rethink many of his priorities. He resolved to rise earlier each day to devote more time to prayer. He emptied his savings account and gave everything to the poor. The change was even reflected in his appearance. Once a portly figure, he gradually took on the more gaunt and monastic look of his later years. It was all part of a quiet process of conversion that transformed a successful churchman into a man of God and prepared him for the trials that were to come.

Beginning in 1993, Bernardin was beset by a series of terrible ordeals. It started with a lawsuit by a one-time seminarian from Cincinnati, who claimed he had been sexually abused by Bernardin, his bishop at the time. Though devastated by this accusation, Cardinal Bernardin responded with calm conviction. He utterly denied the charge, while insisting that his case be investigated by the review board he had established for such allegations. He refused to impugn his accuser's character or do anything that might discourage other victims of abuse from coming forward.

The story soon took an astonishing turn, however. The accuser, who had been counseled by an unlicensed therapist, admitted the "unreliability" of his memories and unreservedly withdrew his charges. Though Bernardin's reputation had been indelibly besmirched, he agreed to meet privately with the young man, who was dying of AIDS, celebrated Mass with him, and offered his forgiveness.

It was a powerful witness of the gospel, seemingly rewarded with a happy ending. But it was only the beginning of Bernardin's Way of the Cross. Not long after his vindication he called a press conference to announce that he had been diagnosed with pancreatic cancer.[40]

Shortly before this announcement, I had met with the Cardinal and his priests. He had written to me just before I was scheduled to go to Guatemala to work with persons ministering to abused and tortured Indians, and asked if

I would speak to a gathering of his priests about self-care. After I gave the talk he expressed his gratitude to me and teased that he would like to sit with me for a session. He also agreed to review a book I was writing. Typical for him, he told me that not only was he willing to do it but that it would be an honor.

After that, we were supposed to get together at my house for dinner some time in the future, but it never happened. He died from pancreatic cancer. However, his kindness to me and to so many others still lives on. But as we just saw in the passage from Robert Ellsberg, he did not take for granted the need to fill himself with what would allow him to remain free for others. Certainly we should not take such things for granted either. In the next chapter we will look at those ways that we can feed our souls but which also continue to increase our hunger.

seven

FEED YOUR SOUL

There are many types of food for the soul that we can explore. They all encourage us to maintain the sense of perspective, openness, and emptiness that we need. In accordance with desert wisdom, such things certainly would include:

- gratitude,
- simplicity,
- a listening spirit,
- appreciation of one's vulnerability,
- recognition of the fragility of life,
- scripture,
- unceasing prayer.

Gratitude

When Abba Benjamin was dying he left those around him this message:

> Do this and you will be saved:
> rejoice always,
> pray constantly,
> and no matter what the circumstances,
> *give thanks*.[41]

Deep gratitude opens us up so we can have a new sense of perspective, no matter what happens in life. People who have this grace are even noteworthy to those who encounter them. The circle of grace formed by their gratitude and the sense of perspective it brings shines through in the simplest of conversations with them.

Once I was invited to visit India to offer some days of spiritual and psychological renewal. I traveled around the state of Bihar, one of the poorest states in India. The group of dedicated Jesuits who serve in different ways there wanted me to help them celebrate the fiftieth jubilee of their foundation. My role was to give presentations in four different settings. Most of the time I traveled by jeep, but sometimes I would travel in an ambulance because it was safer. There had been a hijacking of a bus on one of the roads we had to take, and two people were killed. But those who had invited me said that no one, not even bandits, would stop an ambulance (although I noticed that everyone in the ambulance traveling with us got quiet once we reached the turn in the road where the hijacking had occurred!).

On one of these journeys the day after I had given a daylong workshop, we pulled into a small village where one of their schools was located. I had lunch with some of the men, took a siesta, and afterward went out to experience the beautiful afternoon sun. As I was standing there, one of the men came out to greet me. He was called "the barefoot brother" because he kept misplacing his shoes, although I suspect the real reasons were that he liked walking without them, and each time someone bought him a new pair of shoes he would give them away.

He asked me if I wanted to take a short walk to visit some Catholic nuns who were working in the area, and I said that I would be happy to join him. As we walked along, he inquired, "Would it be too personal for me to ask you about your family?" After I told him, "Not at all." I described my family and then asked him about his.

He had come from a big family. Since his father died young, he said he had to stay at home and take care of the younger children. That was why he entered the Society of Jesus so late in life. When I asked about his siblings, he told one sad tale after another about the tragedies that had befallen many of them—accidental deaths, terminal illnesses, etc.—the list seemed endless. The surprising thing was that he told it in a very matter of fact way that demonstrated acceptance of the different turns in life.

After he had finished his story, but while we were still walking along, he stopped on the dusty road, turned to me with a smile and said, "I must thank you before I forget." Surprised, still in a reverie about how much this man had been through and how calm and at peace he was now, I asked, "Why would you ever be thankful to me?" In response, he said to me with an even broader smile on his face, "Your day of renewal yesterday truly lifted my spirits. It was so good of you to come so far to help us this way." After he said this, I thought I was going to cry. He was thankful to *me*? Given all the good he was doing, the problems he had risen above, and the sense of appreciation he had for literally everything, including my small contribution, he was a gift to me.

Entitlement is one of the greatest dangers to the spiritual life and an enemy to our sense of inner peace. The Jesuit brother had no part in such an attitude. He lived in the now and was open to all that God was giving him. In this respect, gratitude is a perfect example of that which both satisfies us and leaves us open to experience more. When we feed our souls with gratitude we can experience whatever good may come along in a myriad of ways. Brother David Steindl-Rast speaks about this in his book *Gratefulness*. He notes that most of us leave the house each day with a mental list of certain particular things for which we will be grateful. His advice is to discard the list and be grateful for any and all things that come our way.

This alone, if we could do it, would transform our lives and be a constant source of perspective.

Simplicity

Simplicity is another attitude with which to seed our souls so we can live without being torn apart by unnecessary troubles. Most people see simplicity as something external and there are many books to tell us how we can simplify our lifestyles, schedules, and homes. They are helpful to some extent, but it is internal simplicity that will really help us to be free. Even if we have very little or a job that is small, we can still not have simplicity.

The opposite of this is also true. We can have much or be powerful, and yet be simple. A good example is the former Secretary General of the United Nations, Dag Hammarskjöld. He had a very demanding job that took him around the world. He met different dignitaries, encountered representatives following any number of national agendas, and yet there was a simplicity about him. It can be seen in his published journal, *Markings*.

Simplicity also allows us to see the world in ways that prevent us from feeling overwhelmed. When we have inner simplicity, we are better able to offer sound advice when others who are under great stress come to us anxiously looking for "a word." For instance, in the fourth century, one young brother was quite distraught. He was obsessed by many disruptive thoughts and didn't know how to overcome them. In response the Desert Father said:

> Do not seek to take all these thoughts on at the same time. Instead, fight against one. All thoughts have a single source. And so, you simply need to determine what it might be and fight against it. Then, you will be rewarded by defeating the rest of them without lifting another finger to accomplish it.[42]

Simplicity also allows us to more readily recognize when our ego is seducing us or how the culture in which we live is trying to sell us on something that it believes will make us happy—if we buy it! Simplicity also allows us to be a little less busy, a bit more relaxed. We can be active without being preoccupied, pulled down or exhausted by what we are doing. Burnout isn't caused by the amount of work we do as much as by how we view that work. When we are motivated by fear—of failure, of people making fun of us, or of losing something we erroneously believe we need for happiness—we are more likely to burn out. Simplicity is truly the gift that keeps on giving because it allows us to be in a position to see everything as a gift and not to be worried about what is unnecessary or by things that we encounter that are beyond our control.

A Listening Spirit

To be a deep listener is a wonderful thing. We learn so much that it is so very satisfying. At the same time, a listening spirit also helps us to remain open enough so that we don't miss things because of a narrow, preconceived view of life and how we feel it should be. Too often we have set ways of learning and listening that are so narrow that much of the opportunity for learning is lost. For example, one renowned and highly educated Desert Father was found by his apprentices to be speaking at length with a local peasant. Later that evening he was asked by the younger brothers why he, such a learned man who even knew Sanskrit, was speaking to this illiterate worker. In response, he simply replied, "Ah yes, I do know many things. But I know not one word of 'peasant.'"

Strangers, children, coworkers, acquaintances, the list of potential teachers is endless if we have the ears to listen and the eyes to see. Take for example this simple encounter. My mother died in 2004 at the age of ninety-five. When I heard she had died suddenly, I was surprised by how deeply I felt about it. After all, she was ninety-five and had led a full life. I also felt that she seemed so unhappy much of the time, even when things were great and people were so nice to her. Later on, I shared these observations about my grief with my daughter. In response, she said, "Well, she was your mother, Dad, so it doesn't matter how long she lived. Of course you would be sad. Also, I don't think Grandma was truly unhappy. She just wasn't happy in the same way you and I are." My daughter's insights were right on target and were a great gift to me during the time after my mother's death. As I look back through the lens of a listening spirit I am glad I was in a position at that point to hear my daughter's wise words. There is so much I miss when that spirit is lacking.

A listening spirit is also important because it allows us to be open enough to be surprised by life. This once occurred when I was at a liturgy in Baltimore to commemorate and celebrate the anniversary of the founding of the oldest Carmelite convent of Catholic nuns in the United States. It was the closing of Mass, and the choir and musicians struck up a powerful version of the Hallelujah Chorus from Handel's *Messiah* to send us off with a grand sense of joy. Just as the music and singing started, there was some commotion to the right that caught my eye. I turned and saw a group of hearing-impaired persons being led by a man who knew the words to the Hallelujah Chorus and was signing it for those present in that section of the congregation. As I was marveling at his signing, all of a sudden the rest of the hearing-impaired people in the section started signing it with him. They knew it too! On that afternoon, I think I heard the Hallelujah Chorus "sung" more dramatically than ever before. It was the grace of a listening spirit that I was fortunate enough to be blessed with at that moment that allowed this particular rendition of the "Hallelujah Chorus" to be a new experience for me. As a matter of fact, when grace is present, even our vulnerabilities can teach rather than simply deflate us.

Appreciation of One's Vulnerabilities

Our vulnerabilities can teach us wonderful things if we let them. In response to someone who sought his advice, Ranier Maria Rilke wrote a little classic called *Letters to a Young Poet*. In it he wrote:

> Only someone who is ready for everything, who excludes nothing, not even the most enigmatical, will live the relation to another as something alive and will himself draw exhaustively from his own existence. For if we think of this existence of the individual as a larger or smaller room, it appears evident that most people learn to know only one corner of their room, a place by the window, a strip of floor on which they will walk up and down. Thus they have a certain security. And yet that dangerous insecurity is so much more human which drives the prisoner in Poe's stories to feel out the shapes of their horrible dungeons and not be strangers to the unspeakable terror of their abode. We, however, are not prisoners. No traps or snares are set about us, and there is nothing which should intimidate or worry us. . . . We have no reason to mistrust our world, for it is not against us. Has it terrors, they are our terrors; has it abysses, those abysses belong to us; are dangers at hand, we must try to love them.[43]

Perspective is at issue here. We must be willing to use our vulnerabilities as a tool to gain perspective in life. If we do, it will keep us from being pulled into the type of denial that is based on the illusory feeling that change will never challenge us. Even small unexpected events in our life can wake us up to the fact that this is a lie.

I remember going into my basement to see if the drain outside the door was clear of debris. The rain was like a deluge and I was afraid that it might back up and I would have a flood. Just as I got down there, muddy water started rushing under the door. By the time I got the drain cleared, the rug was soaked with mud.

As I cleaned up I was surprised at how helpless I felt trying to stop the water from seeping into the house. When the rain finally stopped I opened up the door to let the basement air out. I also opened a window to let the air flow through. It wasn't until three days later that I realized that unlike the door, the window did not have a screen on it. I had taken it off a few months back to clean it and neglected to put it back on. When I discovered this, I closed the window, looked around to see if anything had gotten in, saw nothing, and thought, "No harm done."

A few days later my wife was in the basement and saw something stuck under the window sash on the *inside* of the house and called me to get a ladder and come down to see what it was. It turned out to be a six-foot snakeskin! Needless to say, I felt vulnerable—not only in theory, but in fact. Later that night as I thought about it, I realized how little events like some mud on the rug and finding a snakeskin can wake us up. We just go through life as if we have forever, that there is nothing that will change our life. Such little vulnerabilities can bring with them perspective, if we are open to their message. But even though they can be powerful in their own way, they are not in the same league as the impending force of our greatest source of vulnerability: death.

Recognition of the Fragility of Life

Thomas Merton once shared a strange experience he had during prayer. It was as if the angel of death rushed by him. The angel didn't stop, but Merton said he felt that he did take note of him. We may have similar experiences, be they dramatic or softly felt.

Recently, I had two of them. I had gone to a funeral for the father of one of the secretaries at Loyola College where I teach. As I entered the chapel and was greeted by her it was as if I could see into the future when my daughter would be greeting people at my wake. I didn't think too much about it until a second experience occurred several weeks later.

In the morning, I have a wonderful ritual that I never tire of experiencing. I get up early—sometime between 4:30 and 6:00 a.m., sit quietly in bed with a cup of coffee for about half an hour. Following this, I get a second cup for myself as well as one for my wife who is usually awake by then. Then we chat for a bit before getting involved in the activities of the day. On this particular morning, I was still on my first cup, sitting quietly, when I noticed a very dimly lit photo of myself on my wife's dresser. It was the one used on the jacket of my book *Riding the*

Dragon. However, instead of thinking it was a nice photo, I thought: "That's the type of photo the family gives to the newspapers when a person dies."

Although the thought may seem morbid, it was a good one for me. Once again, it awakened me to see how I was rushing toward my grave without paying attention to those around me and that I lacked a spirit of gratitude. Contemporary culture would have us deny that death is coming. But it is, and knowing this keeps us aware, appreciative, *open*. We realize that we are dying and so are all those around us. Such a realization has the power to change the way we deal with people if we let it. It also reinforces our gratitude for everything and prevents us from falling into lockstep with a cultural attitude that is always chasing goals. We need to be purged of this pursuit! Instead, as the fourth-century desert monks and nuns learned, we should seek to be fed by what would transform our day and, in turn, our lives, rather than be caught by the compulsions and chains of contemporary life. And what better food for our minds and hearts to encourage this than embracing sacred scripture?

Scripture

The revered desert elder Abba Poemen, once said:

> The nature of water is yielding; whereas, the character of stone is that it is hard. Still, if you suspend a bottle filled with water above a stone so that the water can drip, drop by drop on the stone, eventually it will

wear a hole in the stone. In a similar way the Word of God is so tender, and we are hard-hearted. Yet, when people are able to frequently hear the Word of God, their hearts can be opened and they shall have a sense of awe with respect to God and they will be changed.[44]

Noted Anglican spiritual writer Kenneth Leech describes the importance of scripture this way:

> The desert movement was saturated in the Scriptures, learning whole books by heart. The Desert Fathers held, with Epiphanius of Cyprus, that "ignorance of the scriptures is a precipice and a deep abyss." They used the Psalms constantly. Their prayer was utterly and profoundly biblical. The contemplation of God was inseparable from the response to God's word in revelation, and the deep inner struggle with the heart involved the interiorizing and digesting of the scriptures.[45]

Douglas Burton-Christie in his well grounded and thoroughly researched book, *The Word in the Desert*, further supports these points and notes:

> Private, oral recitations of Scripture was viewed as one of the most effective means of protecting the monk against the snares of the evil one . . . the form that the assault takes is the "stirring up of memories." . . . Meditation on scripture—literally reciting it by heart—not only occupies the memory of the monk but creates a new, potentially healing reservoir of

> thoughts . . . without advocating repression, [scripture] provides . . . a practical strategy for avoiding their fiercest blows.[46]

For us today, scripture plays an equally important role if we are serious about the way we approach it. Our identity should be on the line. As Christian reform theologian Karl Barth warns, when we do a spiritual exegesis of scripture and ask what is this book saying in a particular passage, it should say back to us, who is it that is asking?

A tale told about the mystical *rebbe* Israel Baal Shem Tov illustrates this even more poignantly. When a young man came to him and told him he wished to be a rabbi, the famous *rebbe* told him to go through Torah. Instead of returning years later, he came back in only several months, boldly proclaiming that he had been through Torah twelve times! In return, with sadness in his eyes, the *rebbe* quietly responded, "Yes. But how many times has Torah been through you?" As the deeply spiritual rebbe recognized, when we encounter scripture in a serious, prayerful way, life for and in us changes radically. We can see more clearly, let go more easily, and experience the purity of heart to which all of us are called at each stage of life. But as was described in this encounter, in spiritually embracing scripture, we are not merely reading it. We are praying and living it. In that way it becomes a cornerstone of a life of unceasing prayer that is at the basis of all desert wisdom.

Unceasing Prayer

The essential tenet of the desert when one is confused, challenged, or in the midst of a discernment about what should be done is: pray over it, consult someone wiser, always be hospitable to others, and then we will know and do the right thing. The understanding that is at the basis of this guidance is that one needs, above all, to be truly a person of prayer. This was the crucial element that opened one's spiritual eyes to experience life and God in new and deeper ways.

In his book *Reverence*, Paul Woodruff sought this virtue "in odd places." A conclusion he reached from this pilgrimage was, "If your form of worship or your faith is reverent, so much the better. You know one place to look for reverence. But you should look further, so that you can see how you might share reverence with people who do not worship with you or share your faith."[47]

Seeing and expecting not just reverence but God everywhere was a goal of prayerfulness and unceasing prayer in the fourth-century Egyptian desert. As Alan Jones found out on a visit to modern Egypt, this still remains a goal in monasteries there today:

> My host was Father Jeremiah. It's impossible to tell the age of a bearded Egyptian monk, but Jeremiah seemed very old indeed. The first thing he did was bring me tea and something to eat. Then he said with a deep laugh, "Father, we always treat guests as angels—just in case [they are]!"

. . . The secret of monastic life, at its best, is its apostolic simplicity: simplicity without naiveté. Always in Father Jeremiah's eyes were the twin qualities of compassion and wisdom. I could discern no feeling of spiritual superiority or the claim to special knowledge in him or in any of the monks I met. Being willing to explore the possibility of entertaining angels seemed to me to be both compassionate and perceptive, because it challenges the believer to live in a constant state of expectancy, openness and vulnerability. . . .

It was at this point that I began to see a little more clearly *the way of believing* that I was seeking. It is a *way* of hospitality that involves receiving others as lively images of God or as his possible messengers, regardless of whether they are believers or not. The living receptivity towards others is not dependent on their sharing our beliefs or opinions.[48]

Unceasing prayer then is an ideal example of something that will paradoxically both satisfy yet leave us open and spiritually hungry for more. Of all the approaches, prayer is certainly the ideal way to let go and have the purity of heart to see more.

An Uncluttered View through Clear Air

Obviously, the four questions we have been examining were not only relevant in the fourth century, but can help us in life now—especially in the emotional and spiritual deserts in which we find ourselves. They stimulate us to seek exactly what the *ammas* and *abbas* sought, an unclut-tered life of deep meaning, peace and joy, radical honesty, and true simplicity—all hallmarks of a full life of spiritual wisdom and compassion.

From these original desert encounters, we are left today with living guidance on how to navigate similar terrain in our own lives. Such aids are contained in the sayings (*apophthegmata* in Greek) that were passed from *ammas* and *abbas* to their disciples who were seeking a path to truth. The fact that many of us still turn to them again and again today is, once again, a credit to their enduring relevance. As Columba Stewart points out:

> It is obvious that the sayings of the desert fathers touch modern people in ways that other ancient Christian writings do not. This is not because they are pithy, humorous, or bizarre, although they are sometimes all of those things. What sets the *apophtheg-mata* apart from so much of patristic literature is that they speak from and to experience rather than text or theory; they are practical rather than intellectual. The sayings and the stories in which they are set do not try to pursue a topic as far as may be done, to run a concept to ground and examine it, or to construct an argument. The sayings open up rather than exhaust, suggest rather than describe. Like parables, they are explosive, and where the bits land after the explosion is different each time the stories are told or read. The significance of this quality runs deeper than matters of literary genre: it was not a studied preference for

gnomic statements rather than treatises which gave rise to these sayings. The very form of the *apophtheg-mata* arose from and leads back into the heart of the desert quest. These monks staked everything on the effort to destroy illusion and deception. Their various disciplines were intended to help them cut through the noise of lives hooked on the deceptions, material-ism, and games that have characterized human beings since the Fall. The desert itself gave them a landscape which mirrored what they sought for their own hearts: an uncluttered view through clear air.[49]

This search—for the truth in the desert, for purity of heart, for "uncluttered view through clear air," and for an appreciation of how one ought to live as a result of this quest—requires mentorship. Accordingly, we should be especially interested in the elements of a contemporary "desert apprenticeship" as it is manifested across spiritual traditions. The elements of such a process and relationship are essential for us because on the road to inner freedom we are called to play both mentor and disciple roles at different times. Knowing more about the qualities of a mentor in the spirit of the desert will also allow us to build on what the *abbas* and *ammas* themselves have set before us in their sayings—especially with respect to the value placed on humility, action, and faithfulness on the spiritual journey to experiencing true freedom.

eight

Become a Desert Apprentice

The fourth-century Egyptian desert was more than a barren wasteland—although surely it was that as well. It was seen by the pilgrims who went there to be a place of deep learning, a university of the soul.[50] It was also a place where it was possible to have a spiritual relationship with a unique type of guide:

> At the center of this educational process was the spiritual father, the *pneumatikos pater*. "Where are the great and wise men," Jung once asked, "who do not merely talk about the meaning of life and the world but really possess it?" The holy men of the desert were seen as more than tutors. They were bearers of the spirit, charismatic figures, and between them and their disciples there was a relationship comparable to that of apprenticeship. Thoughts and feelings, the

innermost motions of the heart, were exposed to the spiritual father, as a necessary part of coming to know oneself, to be free of dishonesty, and to mature. "Give me a word, father" is a recurring demand of the desert disciple. Often the response would be a short gospel word to be brooded upon in silence and solitude.[51]

In an essay entitled, "The Spiritual Father in the Desert Tradition," Merton adds this description of the relationship and how the *abba* is essential so the seeds of spiritual growth don't simply lie dormant:

The *abba* or spiritual Father was first of all one who by long experience in the desert and in solitude had learned the secrets of desert life. He was, by reason of his holiness, endowed with charismatic gifts, which enabled him to detect and dispel the illusions that would inevitably tempt the beginner—or even the experienced monk who had not yet fully attained to the full maturity and perfection of the monastic life. But the function implied by the name "Father" is not fully accounted for in spiritual advice and instruction. The spiritual Father exercised a genuine "paternity"—in the name of God—engendering the life of the Spirit in the disciple. Of course, this concept must not be exaggerated (as it has sometimes been in later monastic circles . . .). The only source of the spiritual life is the Holy Spirit. The spiritual life does not come from men. The Holy Spirit is given in Baptism. However, as we know too well, the seeds of the spiritual life planted in Baptism too often remain dormant or die altogether. The *abba* or "spiritual Father" was one who was recognized as a charismatic and "life-giving" influence, under whose care these mysterious seeds would truly grow and flourish. The Fathers attracted disciples who came not only for lectures and counsel, but seeking *life* and growth in a special relationship of filial love and devotion. . . .[52]

For most people today such an intense relationship would be at the very least impractical and, for good reasons, possibly undesirable. However, it would be foolish not to emulate some of the primary facets of the apprenticeship relationship as either the guide or the person seeking some direction. We need help to create the psychological and spiritual room to let go of what is unnecessary and destructive in life and welcome what is good and freeing. No matter what final form the relationship takes today, even though the physical challenges may be less rigorous, it is still not to be taken lightly. Just as in the fourth-century desert, we must:

- be committed to act—not just desire or talk about change;

- know why we are seeking such a psychologically costly mentoring relationship; and

- appreciate what a contemporary *abba* or *amma* should truly be like when we are prepared to take the significant step to seek one or are asked to be such a presence to others.

In examining these three points, we will also see that there are key elements from an array of spiritual traditions upon which we can draw to illustrate them. Desert wisdom is present in all major religions, but in different ways.

Commitment to Act

A *rinpoche* from the Tibetan Buddhist tradition notes, "When you see a person who is, as you say, enlightened, and you wish you would be able to attain these qualities, it is very important that you put this wish into action."[53] Too often people spend their whole adult lives just musing about how nice it would be to have a highly trusted mentor with whom they could share their life in a transparent way. Instead of perpetual musing we need to follow through on the desire to be open with someone wiser and holier than we are.

While we owe a mentor or guide a great deal of respect, we still need to be careful about idol worship. We must keep our eye on the ultimate goal and not on the spiritual guide we believe can help us get there. As the first great poet in the history of haiku, Matsuo Basho, said, "Do not seek to follow in the footsteps of men of old, seek what they sought." Or, once again, in the words of the Desert Fathers, "Seek God, not where God lives."

Once we are willing to act, the next step is to have the most serious commitment to become involved in the process. We must continue to be faithful to it, and not step back—no matter what! To navigate all of this with effort, intensity, and faithfulness is not easy. As writer, photographer, and activist Walter Lippman clearly appreciates, "To want salvation cheap, and most men do, there is very little comfort to be had out of a great teacher." For instance, even when we do feel a sense of being drawn into the relationship, one we have possibly sought for years, the hesitation to take advantage of the gift of finding a true teacher and becoming fully involved with this wise figure may still be there.

We can see this paradox of intimacy in Andrew Harvey's spiritual classic, *Journey in Ladakh*. Speaking of a Tibetan *rinpoche*, one businessman who was also an impetuous spiritual seeker shares the following impression with Harvey as to why he thinks his guide is different: "He makes you feel immediately at home with him. He does not want anything from you. He is tender to all the people around him. . . . You feel seen by him." But later he also confesses: "Men like him are [also quite] frightening. They are so clear they make you feel dirty. For the last twenty years I have been wanting to meet a man like him—and when I did, the first thing I wanted to do was to leave. . . ."[54]

So, even before approaching a spiritual master or sage, we must be willing and appreciative of what is involved. In my book *Touching the Holy* I outlined four factors that are important to remember when we seek out a spiritual guide or mentor:

1. We only seek such special assistance when there is a real need and we have already utilized and found somewhat wanting all existing supports in our lives, including our own personal resources (i.e., problem-solving, reflection, prayer).

2. We need to be serious in our request for information and not just inquisitive (some people are continually asking for "a word" from these spiritual figures without weighing the gravity of their request).

3. Take special care in selecting someone who we feel will be of real benefit to us *now*. There is an old Russian proverb that states: "The hammer shatters glass but forges steel." A sage who can be of real help to one person at certain junctures in life may be of no assistance to him or her at another point or be of no help at all to other types of individuals who seek help. . . .

4. Recognize that we might not like, or immediately understand what we are told . . . even Jesus had many persons who came to him who did not react positively to his answers to their questions.[55]

Although a relationship like this offers the hope of a path to peace and joy, entering into such a relationship is not to be taken lightly. There must be a willingness to deal with questions and suggestions that will be taxing at times. We must be honest, open, and sometimes even courageous and strong. Again, a desert story makes this clear.

Abba Sisoes the Theban requested of his disciple,

"Tell me what you see in me and in turn I will tell you what I see in you."

His disciple said to him: "You are good in spirit but a little harsh."

The old man said in reply:
"You are good in spirit too but your soul is not tough enough."[56]

Why Seek Such a Psychologically Costly Relationship?

Clearly, the road to uncovering and embracing desert wisdom in our lives is not an easy one. It is natural for us to wonder, given all the effort and potentially painful experiences of being a disciple, why we would ever want a desert-type relationship? Well, there are a number of reasons for making such a commitment. One, there is a deep desire to be with someone with whom we can be ourselves: sharing joys and sadness, doubts and convictions, shames and proud moments, questions and philosophies. But underneath all of this is a simple need to re-experience one's life with all of its wishes, fears, anger, impulses, and past significant relationships.

The goal is to recreate one's life, to emotionally, cognitively, and behaviorally restructure the way one journeys through life along more personally satisfying lines. The belief is that as an apprentice I will be able to borrow from the strength as well as the philosophy of someone whom I trust. As an apprentice I believe that my guide is living more authentically and peacefully than others. As a result, by being faithful to the lessons I am taught through word and modeling I can do the same—albeit in a different, maybe lesser, way. As is the case of many types of spiritual and psychological mentoring, it is the *relationship* that is crucial. This very interpersonal connection enables a person to choose differently, act more wisely, and finally make progress rather than being caught in a web of old habits.

We can see this in the Zen tradition as well. Judith Simmer-Brown shares that:

> When I first met my root teacher, Venerable Cho-gyam Trungpa Rinpoche, I asked why a personal teacher was necessary. He answered, "It is because we tend to be too hard on ourselves." If we have a personal teacher who can really see us, it is possible to give up torturing ourselves unnecessarily. In my relationship with Rinpoche, I was often embarrassed because he would see my confusion and self-absorption so clearly, but even more I was constantly overwhelmed by his warmth and compassion toward me.[57]

Still, the essential questions remain:
- Who will serve as this person?
- What traits does one seek in such an individual?

- Are there commonalities among helpers that it would be beneficial to know about when seeking out someone like this?

Knowing and finding the right type of person to guide us can make all the difference. Although the relationship is not the only condition for change, it is certainly a *necessary* condition if significant progress in strengthening our inner life is to become a reality. Similarly, if we are to be a guide for others in either a formal or (as is more often the case) informal way, then we must also be aware of how we are to accompany people seeking a new life.

What Are These People Like?

Obviously there are many traits or gifts that ancient *abbas* and *ammas* had and that contemporary guides should seek to possess. However, for our purposes I would like to briefly focus on several that appear to be quite essential especially given the intensity a mentor-apprentice relationship may exhibit at times. My own experience, the wisdom of different world religions, and the stories from the fourth-century desert indicates that it is important that guides:

- offer acceptance and "space" to those who seek their assistance;

- possess an encouraging and contagious holiness;

- exemplify "extra-ordinariness," humility, transparency, and practicality;

- offer perspective—especially in the darkness;

- demonstrate the paradox of possibility and challenge;

- are "un-self-conscious";

- are able to be at home in the now;

- do not seek answers as much as ways to live more completely with the questions; and

- do not get in the way of the message, remove the person's ultimate independence, or interfere with the movement of the spirit.

Because these traits are so rarely seen today, is it any wonder that finding or becoming such a guide is so challenging? Though this is the case, we must not step back from the call to seek and be what is necessary. There are people like this in the world. In addition, we can and should seek to be like those we admire. We may never reach their spiritual maturity, but it doesn't really matter. What is important is that we strive to be of solace and support to those who ask for our help in the best way we can. And so, spending some time reflecting on the essential qualities of a spiritual guide is a sound next step.

Offer Acceptance and "Space" to Those Seeking Their Assistance

I remember once being with a spiritual guide and thinking "I don't think I aged when I was with him!" Aging takes friction and he was so nondefensive and nonthreatening that I felt like I flowed through the time I was with him. If I had pointed out faults I found in him, I am sure he would have responded: "Why yes. Those are some of my faults. How observant of you to notice." He was an amazing person who had no need for unnecessary defenses and posturing. He was extraordinary and didn't waste energy on defensiveness, but instead had it at his disposal for his own search for self-knowledge as well as the teaching of others like myself who are so bound by our own ego and negative or inadequate training.

The space Desert Fathers and Mothers offered came from the inner space that is reflected in their humility. For instance, Abba John of Thebaid said: "First and foremost, a monk should be humble. In fact, this is the first commandment of our Savior when he said, 'Blessed are the poor in spirit, for theirs is the kingdom of heaven.'"

Such people are ones who embrace solitude, are comfortable with silence, and live out of the final element of the triad of the desert by being persons of unceasing prayer. Their gifts also are "contagious" for those who are open enough to receive the charisms that allow them to be in the world with a sense of true spontaneity, freedom, and purity of heart.

Possess an Encouraging and Contagious Holiness

Someone once said about Zen Master Shunryu Suzuki, "Where he is, is where I want to be in that place of sanity."[58] Much later Mitch Albom, in his best-selling book, *Tuesdays with Morrie*, put the same sentiment forth from a slightly different vantage point by admitting, "When I visited Morrie I liked myself better."[59] Both persons made these statements because there is a unique sense of presence in true spiritual and psychological mentors which is, in itself, transformative.

Jeffrey Kottler addresses this quality of presence in terms of psychotherapy and counseling. His insights can remind wisdom figures and helpers that while they should strive to create this quality of presence, they should also be aware of the great expectations people have when they seek help:

> Lock a person, any person, in a room alone with Sigmund Freud, Carl Rogers, Fritz Perls, Albert Ellis, or any formidable personality and several hours later he will come out different. It is not what the therapist does that is important . . . but rather who she is. A therapist who is vibrant, inspirational, charismatic, who is sincere, loving, and nurturing, who is wise, confident, and self-disciplined will have a dramatic impact by the sheer force and power of her essence. . . .

The first and foremost element of change then is the therapist's presence—his excitement, enthusiasm, and the power of his personality . . . The therapist enters the relationship with clarity, openness, and serenity and comes fully prepared to encounter a soul in torment. The client comes prepared with his own expectations for a mentor, a doctor, a friend, or a wizard.[60]

True guides are people who teach us even more by who they are than by what they know. They are people who enable us to feel that change, *profound* change, in us is possible because of our encounter with them. This can be said about anyone filling a teaching role or a mentoring position. For instance, William James said of college professors, "Organization and method mean much, but contagious human characters mean even more in a university." It is no mere coincidence that his brother, the author Henry James, expressed the following similar sentiment: "A teacher affects eternity, he can never tell where his influence stops."

The presence of contagious holiness not only creates a feeling of support, it also calls us to be open to experience the same holiness but in a unique way in our own lives. In this way, apprenticeship can have a positive ripple effect leading to a stronger spiritual community. A number of years ago, Archbishop Desmond Tutu of South Africa was addressing the divinity students at General Theological Seminary. About half way through his presentation, one of the seminarians in the audience nudged the dean of the seminary who was sitting next to him, pointed up at the stage and said: "Desmond Tutu is a holy man." In response the dean asked, "How do you know that he is holy?" To this the seminarian didn't even blink. Instead, after a brief pause, he replied, "I know that Desmond Tutu is holy because when I'm with Desmond Tutu, *I* feel holy." Can the same be said of us by those who we encounter in our daily lives?

The overall challenge, even when being an apprentice, is to simultaneously ask ourselves specific, potentially revealing questions such as: How do people feel when we are with them? Do they feel the same space of love and freedom given to us by our *ammas* or *abbas*? Or, instead, do they feel our need to control, our desire to be appreciated or followed, our need to be liked or seen as bright, attractive, wise, or holy?

Do they feel this openness and place of safety where they can rest their doubts, problems, and concerns, or do they feel our own anxiety, stress, and defensiveness? What do they feel? If we are filled with ourselves or the desire to be famous, powerful, even effective (as enjoyable as having this wish be granted may be), then we lack the essential ingredient, either *humility, ordinariness*, or in some traditions, *emptiness*.

Exemplify Extraordinariness, Humility, and Practicality

There is a power in true desert *ammas* and *abbas* that comes from their extraordinariness. Trudy Dixon said about Zen Master Shunryu Suzuki:

> The qualities of his life are extraordinary—buoyancy, vigor, straightforwardness, simplicity, humility, joyfulness, uncanny perspicacity . . . but in the end it is . . . the teacher's utter ordinariness [that deepens the student's appreciation of their own spirituality]. Because he is just himself, he is a mirror for his students. . . . In his presence we see our original face and the extraordinariness we see is only our own true nature.[61]

Such a sense of presence is striking. Someone once said of a Benedictine priest who founded a Catholic ashram in India, "To walk into Fr. Bede [Griffiths] was like hitting a wall of holiness."[62] Such individuals have a palpable presence that can have a major impact of its own accord—particularly if the apprentice is ready. As Jack Kornfield in his instructive book, *After the Ecstasy, the Laundry,* notes:

> The understanding of emptiness is contagious. It appears we can catch it from one another. We know that when a sad or angry person enters a room, we too often enter sadness or anger. It shouldn't surprise us then, that the presence of a teacher who is empty, open, awake can have a powerful effect on another person, especially if that person is ripe.[63]

These teachers are ordinary, humble, and able to make the teachings practical and alive since they represent the lessons they impart. Yet they are truly "characters of God" because they build on the sense of magnetism they have in a way that helps people more readily incorporate new and necessary changes into their lives. Sogyal Rinpoche, in his classic work *The Tibetan Book of Living and Dying*, wrote,

> My master, Jamyang Khyentse, was tall for a Tibetan, and he always seemed to stand a good head above the others in a crowd. He had silver hair, cut very short, and kind eyes that glowed with humor. His ears were long, like those of the Buddha. But what you noticed most about him was his presence. His glance and bearing told you that he was a wise and holy man. He had a rich, deep, enchanting voice, and when he taught his head would tilt slightly backward and the teaching would flow from him in a stream of eloquence and poetry. And for all the respect and even awe he commanded, there was humility in everything he did. . . . With his warmth and wisdom and compassion, he personified the sacred truth of the teachings and so made them practical and vibrant with life.[64]

The sense of practicality and common sense Sogyal Rinpoche refers to with respect to his own Master is unfortunately uncommon today. It is a mark of spiritual wisdom that can have a direct impact on a person's life. This is not a new insight. For ages it has been recognized that true wisdom is applicable—even across centuries. The sayings of the Desert Fathers and Mothers being shared in this book certainly point to this reality. In his Introduction to his book on the *Sayings*, Merton emphasizes this for us:

> These words of the Fathers are never theoretical in our modern sense of the word. They are never abstract. They deal with concrete things and jobs to be done in the everyday life of a fourth century monk. But what is said serves just as well for a [modern] thinker. The basic realities of the interior life are there: faith, humility, charity, meekness, discretion, self-denial. But not the least of these qualities of the "words of salvation" is their common sense.[65]

And nowhere is this common sense and the concrete, practical advice they offered more needed than when encountering personal darkness.

Offers Perspective—Even in the Darkness

Thich Nhat Hanh once said, "During the Vietnam War we were so busy helping the wounded that we sometimes forgot to smell the flowers. Night has a very pleasant smell in Vietnam, especially in the country. But we would forget to pay attention to the smell of mint, coriander, thyme and sage."[66] Simple statements like this serve as reminders to stay awake so we can know what gifts lie before us—especially in the most trying of times. This is important because they provide us with a new perspective and way of seeing life.

Still, what they offer is often rejected because it is contained in the seemingly paradoxical combination of possibility and difficulty. In her little book on the Buddha, Karen Armstrong wrote, "[The] life of the Buddha challenges some of our strongest convictions but it can also be a beacon. . . . His example illuminates some of the ways in which we can reach for an enhanced and more truly compassionate humanity."[67]

Thomas Merton, echoes this point in his published journal *A Vow of Conversation*:

> Blakham, writing of [the philosopher] Sartre, says wisely that popular wisdom easily accepts *extreme* views but not *disturbing* ones. The extreme view is that to live well is impossible, or the other extreme that to live well is easy: this they will readily accept. But Sartre's claim that to live well is difficult and possible, they reject as despair."[68]

This is also the core of desert discipleship: to live well, to be free, and to have purity of heart. Then we can see life clearly and completely, we can know that it is both difficult and possible much of the time. Life comes as a single package. It can't be parsed as it often is by those who seek easy answers or want an excuse to shrink from facing the essential questions and challenges that come up for everyone. While there is always challenge, sometimes darkness is unnecessary. With some energy, courage, and guidance from a mentor, darkness can be avoided or turned to our advantage. In my book *Seeds of Sensitivity* I outlined the kinds of darkness that are avoidable and unnecessary. They are important to remember in this context as well:

- lack of self-awareness, self-acceptance, and self-love,

- dishonesty,

- intolerance of others,

- unfinished business with family and friends,

- suppressed/repressed negative feelings,

- poorly-developed ethics, beliefs, and values,

- attachments or addictions,

- hidden, past, or unintegrated embarrassments,

- resistance to intimacy,

- failure to take care of oneself physically,

- lack of honesty and openness in prayer,

- lack of meaning in life,

- ungrieved losses,

- greed,

- unreasonable expectations of self and others,

- a sense of entitlement,

- undealt with anger,

- unwillingness to risk and an inordinate need for security,

- inability to experience quiet in one's life,

- unhealthy self-involvement or, at the other extreme, lack of healthy self-interest,

- failure to set priorities in life,

- irresponsibility,

- being a perfectionist and inordinately self-critical,

- unwillingness to accept love except in ways one has predetermined as meaningful ("if so-and-so doesn't love me then the other warmth and acceptance in my life isn't important"),

- fear of responsibility and a tendency to project blame.[69]

There are of course times when spiritual darkness is unavoidable. Apprentices need to be helped to see this and not run away. There is always the temptation to medicate oneself with drugs, sex, work, or even prayer. It is difficult to be present to this darkness so it can eventually give way to new learning and "light." In the words of one Zen Master when confronted by an upset disciple who was ready to give up, "You try and you try and you fail, and then you go deeper."[70] Just those words enabled the distressed apprentice to remain where he needed to be: with his darkness.

A *Sense of "Un-self-consciousness"*

Characters of God also have a sense of "un-self-consciousness." Their goodness flows naturally and freely, not out of a sense of duty or because of guilt. Henri Nouwen provided a fine example of this when he indicated our limitations with respect to the way we often "love" others. He said:

> It is important for me to realize how limited, imperfect, and weak my understanding of love has been. . . . My idea of love proves to be exclusive: "You only love me truly if you love others less"; possessive: "If you really love me, I want you to pay special attention to me"; and manipulative: "When you love me, you will do extra things for me." Well, this idea of love easily leads to vanity: "You must see something very special in me"; to jealousy: "Why are you now suddenly so interested in someone else and not in me?"; and to anger: "I am going to let you know that you have let me down and rejected me."[71]

We see a similar sentiment expressed in a reflection on this spirit of un-self-conscious giving in a story by Taoist philosopher Chuang Tzu who lived in the fourth and third centuries BC:

> In an age when life on earth was full, no one paid any special attention to worthy men, nor did they single out the man of ability. Rulers were simply the highest branches on the tree, and the people were like deer in the woods. They were honest and righteous

without realizing that they were "doing their duty." They loved each other and did not know that they were "men to be trusted." They were reliable and did not know that this was "good faith." They lived freely together giving and taking, and did not know that they were "generous." For this reason their deeds have not been narrated. They made no history.[72]

This sense of giving naturally and with no desire for anything in return is certainly in the spirit of the Desert Fathers and Mothers. Although they are especially known for what they have said about living in silence and solitude and the value of asceticism, compassion remains at the heart of what they teach. We can see this in some of their sayings, particularly the blunt one that follows:

> One brother presented an *abba* with the following situation and question:

> "There are two brothers. One of them keeps a sense of silence and solitude in his cell, fasting for six days at a time, and disciplining himself quite harshly. The other brother serves the sick. Father, of the two of them, who is more acceptable to God?"

> The *abba* responded: "Even if the brother who stayed in his cell, fasting for six days, and hung himself by the nose, he would not equal the one who serves the sick."[73]

Are Able to Be at Home in "the Now"

Inspirational guides are able to be at home in "the now" as well. This is another rare trait but an essential one in a spiritual guide. Irish novelist James Joyce put it well when he said of one of his characters, "Mr. Duffy lived a short distance from his body." If we are honest with ourselves, isn't that the way most of us live much of the time? However, spiritual guides would teach us that the opposite is necessary for us to be fully alive—no matter what is going on. In his book *The Wooden Bowl*, Clark Strand said about his mentor, Deh Chun:

> When I consider the years of our association, the most remarkable thing is that I cannot recall any particular thing I learned from him. I can't point to a particular conversation we had and say, "Well, you know, then Deh Chun said such and such and everything was clear." At the time *nothing* was clear. When I think back on it now, I realize that his entire teaching consisted of being in the present moment, with nothing else whatsoever added on.

> Being with Deh Chun was like dropping through a hole in everything that the world said was important—education, progress, money, sex, prestige. It was like discovering that nothing else mattered and all I needed was *now*—the moment—to survive. Sitting there in the little house, listening to the water boil, to the twigs crackling in the wood stove, I was temporarily removed from the game. That was the

genius of his teaching, that he could bring forth that transformation without even saying a word.

His was a state of complete simplicity. Like water, the direction of his life was downward, always seeking lower ground.[74]

When Strand went on to describe what Deh Chun's physical setting was, it could easily have been one that would suit a modern day desert *abba* or *amma*.

When I met him he lived in a ramshackle two-room house heated by a wood stove the size of a typewriter. There was no furniture, only a few turned-over crates and several cardboard boxes in which he kept his clothes. His bed consisted of two sawhorses on top of which he had placed a 3 x 5 sheet of plywood and a piece of packing foam. I remember thinking once that this bed suited him perfectly, his body was so light and small.

A similar structure in the other room served as a desk for writing letters and for painting his ink-washed Chinese landscapes. Propped against the back door were spades, a shovel, and a rake, tools he used to tend a plot of land the size of two king-size beds laid end to end. With the exception of tea, soybeans, peanut butter, molasses, and occasional wheat-flour, whatever he ate came from there. . . .

Nowadays, in books on meditation, it has become standard practice to say that your teacher was a mirror that allowed you to see your true self. But that was not my experience with Deh Chun. It was more like floating weightless on the Dead Sea and looking up at an empty sky. There was a feeling of tremendous peace and freedom, but that was all. I didn't know *anything* after I was done. Trying to pin him down on some aspect of meditation was as pointless as trying to drive a stake through the air. He taught one thing and one thing only, and that he taught to perfection: meditation happens now.[75]

Living with the Questions and Instilling Patience in Ourselves

True guides who will help us through our inner deserts are filled with wisdom but are not "answer people." Instead, they call us to live with the questions in a different way. For instance, when questioned, one master said, "If I give you an answer you'll think you understand." Thomas Merton similarly advised, "No one can give you a map. Your terrain is unique . . . just some guidance and courage about how to handle different terrain."

Zen Master Shunryu Suzuki offered a similar caution:

> "If I tell you something you will stick to it, and limit your own capacity to find out for yourself." But, as Katagiri Roshi said, "You have to say something." Because if the teacher says nothing, the students wander about sticking to their habitual ways of being.[76]

So, rather than being answer people true guides move us away from the habit of believing quick answers are the most ideal steps to living fully. Instead, a guide's response may offer us hope that is wrapped in active patience. In one of the entries from the classic *Letters to a Young Poet*, Ranier Maria Rilke advises,

> I want to beg you, as much as I can, dear sir, to be patient toward all that is unsolved in your heart and to try to love the questions themselves, like locked rooms and like books that are written in a foreign tongue. Do not now seek the answers, which cannot be given you because you would not be able to live them. And the point is to live everything. Live the questions now. Perhaps you will gradually, without noticing it, live along some distant day into the answers.[77]

Spiritual Sages Don't Get in the Way of What Is Important

No matter how excellent and holy the teacher is, it is the message, the way, the word, or God that must remain central. Guides know they can offer much to their apprentices "simply" by not getting in the way of the lessons the person needs to learn. As Sogyal Rinpoche notes:

> It cannot be stressed too often that it is the *truth of the teaching* which is the central focus which is all important, and never the personality of the teacher.

This is why Buddha reminded us in the "Four Reliances":

Rely on the message of the teacher, not on his personality;

Rely on the meaning, not just the words;

Rely on the real meaning, not the provisional one;

Rely on your wisdom mind, not on your ordinary, judgmental mind.[78]

There is a tendency to put spiritual guides on pedestals and then to be shocked by their clay feet. By recognizing it is God (or in some traditions "the teaching or the way) that must be the ultimate focus, this can be avoided. We must take care in *both* the selection of our teachers and in looking at the teachings they offer us. As Thomas Merton cautioned, in the search for a full spiritual life we must not be like crows and pick up everything that glitters. Those we see as role models and the teachings we follow must be simultaneously practical and filled with passion. In the end, if they don't change our attitudes and the way we live in a good way, then of what use are they? However, if both the gifts and the teachers are good, then we have an opportunity to embrace and practice what we are taught; this can then lead to a groundbreaking epiphany and a sense of new freedom in our lives. (We must also remember this when others come to us for guidance and care!)

Prayerful Openness and Effort: Guiding Lights to New Freedom

Being open to the truth with a sense of humility and a recognition that there are so many ways in which we are not free is at the heart of the apprenticeship process. As Sogyal Rinpoche once again advises:

> View the teacher as physician.
>
> See oneself as patient.
>
> Understand teachings as medicine
>
> Resolve to follow the teachings for cure.[79]

This is similar to classic desert wisdom. Likewise it is worthy of embrace now when obedience is rare, and the presence of a true selfless sage is an even more uncommon occurrence. Once again, in a colorful story from the fourth-century desert the *abbas* were known to say: "If you see a young person climbing to the heavens by his own will, quickly grab him by the foot and pull him right down so he is grounded for what he is doing of his own accord is not good for him."[80]

American Buddhist teacher Jack Kornfield echoes this theme but with a slightly different emphasis. He notes that awakening depends on:

- openness of the student,
- earnest willingness to discover,
- significant period of practice (purification),

- respect and awe surrounding the master,
- field of consciousness of the master—direct presence of love, freedom and emptiness.[81]

What Buddhists Sogyal Rinpoche and Jack Kornfield are pointing to is the need to be both open and passionate, simultaneously faithful and hopeful. This emphasis on a faithfulness that is unwavering on the part of the guide is an essential element in the apprentice-mentor relationship because there is often a tendency on the part of those seeking help (including many of us) to be doubtful as to whether a guide—or *anyone* for that matter—will really be faithful or of any help to us. This doubt and hesitation can hold us back unless we receive timely encouragement, or in the case of those coming to us, we support them when they shy away from seeking a wisdom figure or following the teachings that will set them free.

Andrew Harvey says, "It is hard to believe in any help." A Tibetan companion wisely responds to this by saying, "That is because you have not found out where help is."[82] For each of us this person is someone who has a particular gift that will help release us from the inner chains that remain and be able to nourish the seeds of the spiritual life that are presently dormant in us.

The Charism of the Guide

People have a particular gift or charism out of which they live. When we are exposed to this gift we are pulled in by it—for good or for bad. Millicent Dillon, in her infatuating biography of writer-composer Paul Bowles, notes:

> Something about Paul, about being with him, made one feel that with him you were at the center of the world—his world, maybe even *the* world. How this was created, I don't know. But it was obviously felt not only by me but also by those who clustered about him. It was there, palpable in the air. . . .[83]

The guides who have a dramatic impact on us have found a way to share their charism in a very powerful way. If we are to have an equal impact on our apprentices, we must do the same. Jeffrey Kottler writes, in his book on being a therapist, that even the philosophy or theory of guiding others is attributable to this underlying personal charism. He notes:

> All effective therapists intuitively find a way to capitalize on the strength of their character. [Sigmund] Freud's self-analytic skills, [Carl] Roger's genuineness, [Albert] Ellis's capacity for rational thinking, [Fritz] Perls' playfulness, found the nucleus for their respective theories.[84]

The same can be said of recognized spiritual guides. In addition, we can recognize the power of their charism because it should also lead us to a place of wholeness and holiness that they should all have in common. For instance, "theologians tell us of the themes of different spiritual writers (e.g., Ignatius [of Loyola]—obedience,

Francis [of Assisi]—poverty, [Henri] Nouwen—peace), but are quick to add that by delving deeply into one school of spirituality, we are put into contact with others."[85]

Speaking of the poet Carl Sandberg, American philosopher and painter Edward Steichen said, "When God made Carl, he didn't do anything else on that day." I feel there are a number of people we encounter (in person and in their writings) about whom we might have the same sentiment. Some of these notable persons—and the themes ("words") that they are known for—who quickly come to mind for me are:

Thomas Merton—truth

Henri Nouwen—vulnerability

Mother Teresa of Calcutta—faithfulness

Abraham Joshua Heschel—wonder and awe

Pema Chödrön—courage

Bede Griffiths—trust

Shunryu Suzuki—change

Metropolitan Anthony of Sourozh (Anthony Bloom)—passion

Paramahansa Yogananda—divine intimacy

Dalai Lama—tranquility

Dorothy Day—peace and justice

Anthony de Mello—freedom

Naturally, there are many others we can come up with when asked who has influenced us in person or via their writings. Each of us who has read or been in contact with such characters of God have no doubt been inspired by them, but *inspiration is not enough*. We must absorb their words and then put them into action!

Practice, Practice, Practice

Despite the power of their messages and personages, the *ammas* and *abbas* of the fourth-century desert and the other contemporary guides noted still indicate that, in the end, much rests with the disciple, apprentice, or student as to how transformative an exposure to such figures and lessons will be. As Sogyal Rinpoche recognizes, "One of the greatest things to model is being a student all of your life of the great masters." However, he goes on to caution, "You may have the *karma* (the law of moral effect) to find a teacher, but you must then create the *karma* to follow your teacher."[86]

This requires more than quick action. Sensitive, intuitive awareness of the spirit and the knowledge of the teaching or teacher is also essential. We must appreciate not only the words of the guides who inspire us, but also listen to the attitude or life flow behind their words as well. Anthony de Mello, in speaking of the insightful dialogues he had garnered from many traditions in his book *One Minute Wisdom* cautioned nonetheless:

> This, alas, is not an easy book! It is written not to
> instruct but to Awaken. Concealed within its pages
> (not in the printed words, not even in the tales, but in
> its spirit, its mood, its atmosphere) is a Wisdom which
> cannot be conveyed in human speech. . . . That is what
> Wisdom means: To be changed without the slightest
> effort on your part, to be transformed, believe it or not,
> merely by waking to the reality that is not words, that
> lies beyond the reach of words.[87]

This is exactly what the characters of God convey to
those who interact with them personally. It is what we
can expect if we bring the right motivation and effort to
our encounters with these ancient and modern wisdom
figures—especially if it is not an in-person encounter.

If we are reading their words, we must read, underline,
write out what we've underlined, study, think, learn, over-
learn, over-over-learn, absorb, practice, and then begin
looking at it again as if we were children. The last several
points are especially essential—whether it is through reading or actual contact with a sage. We must employ what
we have learned. If the teachings are to become deeply
rooted, we need to *practice, practice, practice* with those
people (family, friends, coworkers, acquaintances, and
especially those with whom we normally don't get along
or who challenge us) who are in front of us everyday. We
also need to experiment with new behaviors and attitudes
learned with strangers who don't have a habitual response
to us and can further help us build our new practice.

Such practice, if it is good, will soften our souls. It will make us embrace everything that comes our way so the fruits can be good for us and those with whom we interact. In place of grasping, there will be freedom; in place of confusion, greater clarity and simplicity; in place of anxiety, more peace and a greater sense of inner ease. It is not that we will never experience pain, but how we deal with it will be different. No matter how much painful reality comes our way, we will be able to say with confidence, "I really don't have a care in the world." Truly that is the pearl of great price. Seeking this pearl has led to great wisdom, not only in the fourth-century Egyptian desert, but in other times and places as well. Different world religions share with Christianity this quest for inner freedom, and so, the spiritual teachings of all serious seekers are worthy of reflection and practice as a way of making ancient and modern wisdom even more part and parcel of our contemporary lives.

There is, however, one final caution about practice. Often when the practice we are involved in doesn't bring the immediate or exact results we wish, we feel that we have failed. This negative feeling doesn't take into consideration the overall value and positive impact of good spiritual practice designed to rid us of bad habits. Shunryu Suzuki addresses this well in a reflection on Buddhist practice and his own life that he shared with his students. Since it brings to the fore two essential spiritual themes (practice and humility) to recall and repeatedly meditate on, particularly in the deserts of life, it is a fitting one with which to close this chapter.

My own habit is absentmindedness. I am naturally very forgetful. Even though I started working on it when I went to my teacher at the age of thirteen, I have not been able to do anything about it. It is not because of old age that I am forgetful [now], it is my tendency. But working on it, I found that I could get rid of my selfish way of doing things. If the purpose of practice and training was just to correct your weak points, I think it would be almost impossible to succeed. Even so, it is necessary to work on them, because as you work on them, your character will be trained, and you will become free of ego.

People say I am very patient, but actually I have a very impatient character. My inborn character is very impatient. I don't try to correct it any longer, but I don't think my effort was in vain, because I studied many things. I had to be very patient in order to work on my habit, and I must be very patient when people criticize me about my forgetfulness. "Oh, he is so forgetful, we cannot rely on him at all. What should we do with him?"

My teacher scolded me every day: "This forgetful boy!" But I just wanted to stay with him. I didn't want to leave him. I was very patient with whatever he said. So I think that is why I am very patient with others' criticism about me. Whatever they say, I don't mind so much. I am not so angry with them. If you know how important it is to train yourself in this way, I think you will understand. . . . This is the most important point in our practice.[88]

nine

TAKE THREE STEPS
TO INNER FREEDOM

The concept of being given a word, so valued in the fourth-century desert and of a great import for us today, is also really a tool to find out who we truly are and how we are being called to live out our brief lives. Such a process can be very elusive though—even if we are doing what we believe is admirable. Writer, teacher, and activist Parker Palmer recognized this about himself. In his simple yet powerful book *Let Your Life Speak*, he admits:

> When it is clear—if I have eyes to see—that the life I am living is not the same as the life that wants to live in me . . . I [start] to understand that it is indeed

possible to live a life other than one's own. . . . I had simply found a "noble" way to live a life that was not my own, a life spent imitating heroes instead of listening to my heart.[89]

In the desert, this point was made more simply: If you want to find rest here and hereafter, say on every occasion, "Who am I?" and don't judge anyone else. In this complex world with so many demands and insecurities, only those who have a sense of simplicity, single-heartedness, and knowledge of who they are will have a spontaneous, transparent heart which will allow them to *flow* with life rather than drift with it.

At times we can see this quite clearly in little children. Once when we were visiting our daughter and her family, where the guest room is across from the bedroom that our two granddaughters share, the older of the two, Kaitlyn, awoke and was calling out to her mother to come into her room. Soon it became evident that mommy was confident that if something was up, the visiting grandparents would handle it for her, so my wife crossed the hall to Kaitlyn's room to see what she wanted.

As she entered the room, the sun was just rising, and little Kaitlyn, with her elbows leaning on the windowsill, was looking out the window. When she saw my wife, she burst into a smile and said to her in an excited voice, "Look Mom-Mom! God is coloring the sky again." Her unabashed passion and joy showed that she was truly and un-self-consciously being herself. She possessed a natural, deep gratefulness for this wondrous (but daily) gift of God.

We can also see it in adults when they are without guile, fully alive, and simply being themselves in a free and open way. The department chair who preceded me at the university where I teach, a Lutheran minister, was such a person. He was both a passionate and pastoral individual. He also had little quirks that made him even more fun. For instance, whether it was his past history as a pastor or not, he was, shall we say, "a good keeper of the funds." So, it surprised me when he said to me, "Bob, you are going to be chairperson soon, so I think we can justify spending money from the budget to go out to eat to celebrate my passing of the torch to you." In response, I said, "Really? You mean dinner out, Jack?" "No, Bob. *Lunch.*"

When we got to the restaurant, before we ate, I asked Jack if he would like to say grace. He smiled, nodded, and then proceeded to belt out a grace before meals in such a booming voice that everyone stopped talking and put down their knives and forks. (I even think that a couple in the corner who were planning on having an affair at that point changed their minds!) What a wonderful, irrepressible man he was. He obviously knew who he was and lived out of this knowledge without a concern for image or success. He died recently and is missed by all who had the privilege of knowing him.

All of us may feel this sense of freedom and spontaneity at certain times in our lives—maybe at Christmas, a family gathering, after a period of time alone in prayer, or during a quiet walk in the woods. These times point to the fact that a sense of inner freedom is possible for all of us. Yet, we must be more intentional, focused, and willing to expend the energy if we truly desire this pearl of great price.

If we do, two questions arise: How do we become like this? And, what actions must we take in order to find ourselves and then freely share what we find with others? This sense of freedom is what the Jewish tradition calls *mitzvah*, giving and expecting nothing in return. As a way of encouraging reflection on how to respond to these questions, three steps or stages are briefly noted in this last chapter on letting go. These are the steps we need to take when called upon by God.

What mattered most to the fourth-century desert dwellers was knowing who you are and how you should live, so that the fruits of your practice would be bountiful for everyone you met. With this intent in mind, persons were guided to be where they should be and "do the work they needed to do first" before moving on to each next step. The same applies here. To speak about these steps before people are experiencing them is not usually a good idea. The danger is that people will see them as steps on a ladder to perfection or as hoops through which it is necessary to jump. This may lead to an unproductive desire to move through them more quickly than is advisable. Instead it is important to be in the ideal place that God calls you to be at any given point in time. You will know that you're being called to the next step when you no longer feel at home in the place where you are.

It is also helpful to remember that purity of heart is not experienced after we reach the final step. The only way it is possible to experience the true clear vision that will give us rest (*quies*) is by letting go of our own will and being where God wants us to be now. In this light, and this is very important, purity of heart is possible *at each step* if that is where we are supposed to be. Staying back or moving ahead because of our own will actually runs the risk of interfering with the movement of God in our lives. With these caveats, knowing the steps is helpful as a rough guide to consider and adapt given your own spirituality and approach to letting go in order to see yourself, your life, and God as clearly as possible wherever you are *now*.

Step One: Finding Your True Name

There is a story about the Bantu tribesmen that describes how they creep quietly into the rooms of their children when they are asleep and softly whisper in their ears, "Become what you are."[90] As an adult, finding the name God has given us, a "word" to describe ourselves, is a process. We allow God to whisper in our ear and come to recognize our true name through a conscious deliberate process. We don't just drift into an identity given to us by our culture or family environment. Undertaking this task is quite straightforward and simple. Though following it can meet with much resistance in ourselves and/or in our surroundings.

To begin a discernment about the name or charism at the core of our spiritual identity, we need to look for sources of information as to what our gifts are and the one theme, word, or name that could summarize them for us. We can discover this information in a number of ways:

- in quiet prayer, being attuned to the divine stirrings of our own heart,

- by listing our talents and gifts and looking for a common thread running through them,

- asking family, friends, and coworkers, who know us best, what they think represents our gifts and the one word that they feel would summarize our sense of presence to them,

- Inquiring the same of a mentor or counselor who is familiar with our life and personality.

Once the word, theme, or name is chosen, trying it out will help us to determine whether it is truly apt or needs to be altered or changed. For example, initially "enthusiasm" might seem to be the best way to describe our gifts. Only later might we turn to the word "passion" and sense that word is more correct for some reason.

After we find the most suitable word or name, the process doesn't end there. It's just beginning! Our goal is to do everything possible to show gratitude for our gifts and our overarching identity by feeding them, sharing them, and doing whatever we can to almost push those gifts into the realm of magic! When we do this, we may feel, perhaps for the first time, that we are flowing and living out of a life that is truly our own rather than one fashioned by someone or something external. This is truly an experience of living as we were made to live, in the image and likeness of God, the *imago Dei*. Experiencing oneself as *imago Dei* allows life to flow in a way that feels so extraordinarily natural that the creative energy, formerly sapped off in defensiveness, now becomes available to us so that we can, in turn, be available to others.

But, there comes a time when we will recognize that staying on this step—as blessed as it originally was—is in some ways becoming less fulfilling, perhaps even problematic. We may see this in the quality of our presence to others. When we sense this we know it is time to move on and take the next step. But this next step is not the usual way of moving forward that society would hold out to us, and so it may feel a little uncomfortable at first.

Step Two: Find a Second Word

At a certain point, we may begin to recognize that the light which shines as our core energy is too bright or too dim. For instance, if we are passionate, we may sense that there are times when we are intrusive, take up too much interpersonal space, and control rather than inspire others. Or, if we see ourselves as a quiet, listening spirit, able to inspire people with our calm supportive presence, we may begin to sense that we are seen as too shy, fearful, or unwilling to share our opinions or wisdom. It is at this point, after we have tried with all in our power to develop our true selves, we may find we are being called to go against our intuitive movement forward in developing our gifts, theme, or word. Because at this point we are now called to take a step *backward* into our shadow.

More specifically, we are now being called to look for a second word that will buff or soften the first. In the case of passion, the word may be gentle. If our word is listener, maybe the second word is assertive. This new word is not meant to balance out our charism so that it loses its powerful presence and expression in the lives of others. Rather it is designed to help our central gift and identity come across in a way that is most beneficial and generative now that it has already been developed to its maximum.

When we do this, the second word helps us live in a way that is more attentive to others and helps us at a deeper level to lay our ego down rather than to become filled with it. But even this step, which may take years and often is only possible developmentally in our forties and fifties, is still not the final one.

There may come a time when we feel that buffing our first word is not enough. It feels artificial, not completely right. The sense is that God is calling us to be truly *more*. Importantly, this is *not* driven by the superego, i.e., we are not motivated by a voice that says, "I ought to do this to be a better person." Surprising though it may seem, it is also not fueled by the inner desire to be a better person—although certainly that is a good sentiment. It is pure calling. Pure grace.

It is like the experience in the Hebrew scriptures where Abram is called out of his small world to become Abraham, the father of his people, and where his wife Sarai is called to become Sarah, a woman filled with new potential. The calling must be there. One misstep is to move in this direction before you are called. But the real danger is to ignore this call because it requires an even more dramatically different type of step than step two. It requires an actual *leap*.

Step Three: Take a Leap of Faith

The movement of the third step is marked by deep faith. Anthony de Mello offers the following dialogue that provides a sense of what this step is about:

> "Make a clean break with the past and you will be enlightened," said the Master.
>
> "I am doing that by degrees."
>
> "Growth is achieved by degrees. Enlightenment is instantaneous."
>
> Later he said, "Take a leap! You cannot cross a chasm in little jumps."[91]

So, at this point, what is this leap into faith, this jump into the darkness? It is simply this: Take the second word and make it the first. If we are people of passion, then we become gentle first and let the passion come out through that gentleness. If we are deep listeners and our second word is assertive then we are called to move out of ourselves and become assertive first. In other words, while we simultaneously remain a sensitively aware person, we must first take action. The implications for this are obvious. It is not just a major change, although it is certainly that. More accurately, it is a transformation, a true conversion experience.

It also relates to our experience of God and others. If we are a feeling person and our second word is thinking, this step requires us to seek the divine through our intellect. Exploring the left side of the brain allows us to find God in new ways. The impact is also felt in our relationships with others. Just as there is no such thing as a private sin, defensiveness, or bad *karma* that doesn't impact others, the same can be said about the positive steps we make toward God and freedom in responding to the call to take this step. Although this step can happen whenever God wills it, at any time, I have seen it often come during female and male menopause, or after a traumatic experience when new possibility dawns amidst chaos.

Letting Go, Purity of Heart, and the Three Steps

In speaking about all three steps, but especially the last one, we are not just speaking about self-improvement, growth, or even actualization. We are speaking about nothing less than transcendence. We are moving toward the freedom of being who we are called to be so we can live with meaning, peace, and joy by way of purity of heart.

A central tenet of this book has been that this is a change that may come more often than not in the deserts of life or the quiet periods after such trials when we feel lost and a bit numb. But they are not changes that come lightly. They cannot be forced, and it is very possible that the call can be ignored and remain dormant. When that happens, there can be negative consequences and much lost time. The paradigm of the four questions and three steps presented in this book is an effort to demonstrate how this can be avoided or ameliorated whenever possible.

In essence, we are all faced with the question of whether we will be awake and sensitive enough to hear the call, to leave our normal way of interacting, to live and see in new ways with the grace we have been given, and to respond wholeheartedly to God's invitation.

A final caution though: while all of the apprenticeship experiences described in this book have a definite value, they are not meant to replace in any way the subtle grace of God. They are instead really meant to help us answer the question: once graced by God, are we showing gratitude through seeing, embracing, and acting upon these divine gifts?

Once again, a dialogue from de Mello's book of spiritual encounters that was written very much in the spirit of the sayings of the Desert Fathers and Mothers and illustrates this well:

> "Is there anything I can do to make myself Enlightened?"
>
> "As little as you can do to make the sun rise in the morning."
>
> "Then of what use are the spiritual exercises you prescribe?"
>
> "To make sure you are not asleep when the sun begins to rise."[92]

There is a delicate balance in life in which we must know that there are things we can do *and* things beyond our control that we cannot do. In focusing on these steps we are acknowledging all of the information and guidance gleaned from the fourth-century desert Fathers and Mothers and the other spiritual guides and traditions referred to in this book. There is a need for guidance. We can't do it by ourselves. Maybe our periods of apprenticeship will be interspersed with times when books are our only guide. Maybe we will find our guidance informally through wise figures we know and respect. Possibly, it will be a more formal relationship at some point. However, we must not try to do it alone.

Also, just as we let go and move through these steps, others are doing so as well. Part of our movement through them includes a willingness to be present to others who need guidance and may profit by our experience. A sense of community must be present if progress in the spiritual life is to be made. It is not just any kind of community, but one marked by humility and a combination of clarity and kindness so that feedback is given and received without punishment or hidden agendas.

A final recognition, once again, must be noted: these steps are most often taken during or right after desert periods when the foundation of one's life has been shaken. But as one might imagine, the journey isn't mandatory. The many disillusioned, resentful, and jaded people in the world are evidence that there is a great danger that one will not take that step forward when being called by God out of their darkness into new light.

However, if the call to let go of the old and the familiar is responded to when the time is ripe then incredible freedom and love are possible. Persons with a transparent soul can truly flow, rather than drift or fight, with their life. We need only look at the saints, both those proclaimed by the church and the ordinary saints we know in life as proof of this. We need only take the leap to experience it ourselves. The obvious question is *Will we*? This book on humility, letting go, desert apprenticeship, and transparency of soul, has been written to encourage that *yes* be the answer to that question.

NOTES

Introduction

1. Thomas Merton, *Wisdom of the Desert* (New York: New Directions, 1960), 22, 23.
2. Henri J. M. Nouwen, Introduction to Yushi Nomura, *Desert Wisdom* (New York: Doubleday, 1982), xiv-xvii. Italics added.
3. Thomas Merton, *No Man Is an Island* (New York: Doubleday, 1967), 106.

1. Let the Desert Teach You

4. William Langewiesche, *Sahara Unveiled* (New York: Random House, 1996), 7.
5. Alan Jones, *Soulmaking* (San Francisco: Harper, 1985), 12.
6. Quoted in Janet Wallach, *Desert Queen* (New York: Doubleday, 1996), 34. Italics added.
7. Author's translation. Here and elsewhere, when thus cited, the author has translated, paraphrased, or adapted the sayings of the Desert Fathers and Mothers from the following sources: J.P. Migne, ed., *Patroligia Latina*, Vol. 73, (Paris: Garnier, 1849); Thomas Merton, *Wisdom of the Desert* (New York: New Directions, 1960); Yushi Nomura, *Desert Wisdom* (New York: Doubleday, 1982); or Benedicta Ward, *Sayings of the Desert Fathers* (Kalamazoo, MI: Cistercian Publications, 1975).
8. Merton, *Wisdom of the Desert*, 6.
9. Ibid., 24.
10. Author's translation. Italics added.

2. Seek What Is Essential

11. Merton, *Wisdom of the Desert*, 8.
12. Benedicta Ward, *Sayings of the Desert Fathers* (Kalamazoo, MI: Cistercian Publications, 1975), 7.
13. Clark Strand, *The Wooden Bowl* (New York: Hyperion, 1998), 2.
14. Douglas Burton-Christie, *The Word in the Desert* (New York: Oxford University Press, 1983), 78, 89, 91.
15. Merton, *Wisdom of the Desert*, 8.

16. Burton-Christie, *The Word in the Desert*, 158.
17. Donald Brazier, *Zen Therapy* (New York: Wiley, 1995). 13, 14. See also Robert J. Wicks, *Riding the Dragon* (Notre Dame, IN: Sorin Books, 2003).

3. *Enter Through the Narrow Gates*

18. Samuel Dresner, ed., *I Asked for Wonder* (New York: Crossroad, 1986), vii.
19. Author's translation.
20. Anthony de Mello, *One Minute Wisdom* (New York: Doubleday, 1986), 35.
21. Nomura, 27.

4. *Listen to Friends*

22. The first time I discussed this was in *Touching the Holy*.
23. Robert Coles, quoted in Rosalie Riegle, *Dorothy Day: Portraits of Those Who Knew Her* (Maryknoll, NY: Orbis, 2003), 140.
24. I first heard this story told by David Augusburger of Fuller Theological Seminary at the 1991 Religious Education Congress in Los Angeles.
25. Story shared with me by Pamela S. Lowe.

5. *Be Grateful*

26. Ruth Marcus, ed., *The Wisdom of Heschel* (New York: Farrar, Straus and Giroux, 1970), 35.
27. John Berger, *Ways of Seeing* (New York: Penguin, 1977), 146.
28. Shunryu Suzuki quoted in *To Shine One Corner of the World,* ed. David Chadwick (New York: Broadway, 2001), 3.
29. Norman Fischer, quoted in *Benedict's Dharma*, ed. Patrick Henry (New York: Riverhead, 2001), 191.

6. *Ask the Four Desert Questions*

30. Jones, *Soul Making*, 146.
31. Abraham Joshua Heschel, *Man Is Not Alone* (New York: Farrar, Straus and Giroux, 1955), 186, 189.
32. Author's translation.
33. Author's translation.

34. Author's translation.
35. Joseph Goldstein, quoted in *Benedict's Dharma*, 12.
36. Kenneth Leech, *Experiencing God* (New York: Harper and Row, 1985), 154, 155.
37. Robert J. Wicks, *Simple Changes* (Notre Dame, IN: Thomas More/Sorin Books, 2000), 9.
38. Robert J. Wicks, *Overcoming Secondary Stress in Medical and Nursing Practice* (New York: Oxford University Press, 2006).
39. Daniel Mason, *The Piano Tuner* (London: Picador, 2003), n.p.
40. Robert Ellsberg, *The Saints' Guide to Happiness* (New York: Farrar, Straus and Giroux, 2003), 162.
41. Author's translation. Italics added.
42. Author's translation.
43. Ranier Marcia Rilke, *Letters to a Young Poet* (New York: Norton, 1954), 68, 69 .
44. Author's translation.
45. Leech, *Experiencing God,* 140.
46. Burton-Christie, *The Word in the Desert,* 123, 125.
47. Paul Woodruff, *Reverence* (New York: Oxford University Press, 2001), 47.
48. Jones, *Soulmaking,* 13, 14.
49. Columba Stewart "Radical Honesty about the Self: The Practice of the Desert Fathers," *Sobormost* 12 (1990): 25.

8. *Become a Desert Apprentice*

50. Leech, *Experiencing God,* 19, 39.
51. Ibid., 136.
52. Thomas Merton, "The Spiritual Father in the Desert Tradition," *Merton and Hesychasm,* ed. Gray Henry and Jonathan Montaldo (Louisville, KY: Fons Vitae, 2003), 288.
53. Sandy Johnson, *The Book of Tibetan Elders* (New York: Riverhead, 1996), 29.
54. Andrew Harvey, *Journey in Ladakh* (Boston: Houghton-Mifflin, 1983), 125, 135.
55. Wicks, *Touching the Holy,* 119.
56. Author's translation.
57. Judith Simmer-Brown in *Benedict's Dharma,* 97.
58. David Chadwick, *The Crooked Cucumber* (New York: Broadway, 2000), n.p.
59. Mitch Albom, *Tuesdays with Morrie* (New York: Doubleday, 1997), 55.

60. Jeffrey Kottler, *On Being a Therapist* (San Francisco: Jossey-Bass, 1986), n.p.
61. Chadwick, *The Crooked Cucumber*, n.p.
62. Shirley du Boulay, *Beyond the Darkness* (New York: Doubleday, 1998), 252.
63. Jack Kornfield, *After the Ecstasy, the Laundry* (New York: Bantam, 2000), 79.
64. Sogyal Rinpoche, *The Tibetan Book of Living and Dying* (San Francisco: Harper, 1992), xi, xii.
65. Merton, *Wisdom of the Desert*, 13.
66. "An Interview with Thich Nhat Hanh, Vietnamese Zen Master," *Common Boundary*, Nov/Dec, 1989, 16.
67. Karen Armstrong, *Buddha* (New York: Penguin, 2000), xxviii-xxxix.
68. Thomas Merton, *A Vow of Conversation* (New York: Farrar, Straus and Giroux, 1988), 10.
69. Robert J. Wicks, *Seeds of Sensitivity* (Notre Dame, IN: Ave Maria Press, 1995), 127, 128.
70. Chadwick, ed., *To Shine in One Corner of the World*, 15.
71. Henri J. M. Nouwen, *The Genesee Diary* (New York: Doubleday, 1970), 84.
72. Thomas Merton, *The Way of Chuang Tzu* (New York: New Directions, 1965), 76.
73. Author's translation.
74. Strand, *The Wooden Bowl*, 7, 8.
75. Ibid., 8, 9.
76. Shunryu Suzuki, *Not Always So* (New York: Harper Collins, 2002), viii.
77. Rilke, *Letters to a Young Poet*, 34, 35.
78. Rinpoche, *The Tibetan Book of Living and Dying*, 130.
79. Ibid., 130.
80. Author's translation.
81. Kornfield, *After the Ecstasy, the Laundry*, 80, 81.
82. Harvey, *Journey in Ladakh*, 167.
83. Millicent Dillon, *You Are Not I: A Portrait of Paul Bowles* (Los Angeles: University of California Press, 1998), 27.
84. Kottler, *On Being a Therapist*, n.p.
85. Robert J. Wicks, *Availability* (New York: Crossroad, 1986), 23.
86. Rinpoche, *The Tibetan Book of Living and Dying*, 132.
87. de Mello, *One Minute Wisdom*, 2, 3.
88. Suzuki, *Not Always So*, 92.

9. Take Three Steps to Inner Freedom

89. Parker Palmer, *Let Your Life Speak* (San Francisco: Jossey-Bass, 2000), 2, 3.
90. Norman Fischer, *Taking Our Places* (San Francisco: HarperCollins, 2003), 2.
91. de Mello, *One Minute Wisdom*, 36.
92. Ibid., 11.

Selected Bibliographies

Desert Wisdom

Anson, P.F. *The Call of the Desert: The Solitary Life in the Christian Church*. London: SPCK, 1973.

Athanasius. *The Life of Antony and the Letter of Marcellinus*. Translated and introduced by Robert C. Gregg. New York: Paulist Press, 1980.

Brown, Peter. "The Rise and Function of the Holy Man in Late Antiquity." *Journal of Roman Studies 61* (1971). Reprinted with revisions in *Society and the Holy Late Antiquity*. Berkeley: University of California Press, 1982.

Burton-Christie, Douglas. *The Word in the Desert*. New York: Oxford University Press, 1993.

Chitty, D.S. *The Desert a City*. Crestwood, NY: SVS Press, 1977.

Cox, Patricia. *Biography in Late Antiquity: A Quest for the Holy Man*. Berkeley: University of California Press, 1983.

Cassian, John. *Conferences*. Translated by Colm Luibheid. Introduced by Owen Chadwick. CWS. New York: Paulist Press, 1985.

Chrysostomos, Archimandrite. *The Ancient Fathers of the Desert*. Brookline, MA: Hellenic College Press, 1980.

Ellsberg, Robert. *The Saints' Guide to Happiness*. New York: Farrar, Straus and Giroux, 2003.

Entralgo, P. Lain. *The Therapy of the Word in Classical Antiquity*. New Haven: Yale University Press, 1970.

French, R.M., trans. *The Way of the Pilgrim*. New York: Seabury Press, 1965.

Gould, Graham. "The Desert Fathers on Personal Relationships." Ph.D. dissertation, Cambridge University, 1988.

Gruen, Anselm. *Heaven Begins within You: Wisdom from the Desert Fathers*. New York: Crossroad Publishing, 1994.

Hamilton, Andrew. "Spiritual Direction in the *Apophtheg-mata*." *Colloquium* 15 (1983).

Hannay, J. *The Wisdom of the Desert*. London: Methuen, 1904.

Heschel, Abraham Joshua. *Man Is Not Alone*. New York: Farrar, Straus and Giroux, 1955.

Jones, Alan. *Soul Making: The Desert Way of Spirituality*. San Francisco: Harper and Row, 1985.

Kottler, Jeffrey. *On Being a Therapist*. San Francisco: Jossey-Bass, 1986.

Leech, Kenneth. *Experiencing God: Theology as Spirituality*. New York: Harper and Row, 1985.

Louth, Andrew. *The Wilderness of God*. Nashville: Abingdon Press, 1991.

Mayers, Gregory. *Listen to the Desert: Secrets of Spiritual Maturity from the Desert Fathers and Mothers*. Liguori, MO: Triumph Books, 1996.

Merton, Thomas. "The Spiritual Father in the Desert Tradition." *Cistercian Studies* 3 (1968).

———. *The Wisdom of the Desert*. New York: New Directions, 1960.

Nomura, Yushi. *Desert Wisdom: Sayings from the Desert Fathers*. Introduction by Henri Nouwen. Garden City, NY: Doubleday and Company, 1982.

Nouwen, Henri. *Way of the Heart*. New York: Seabury/Harper, 1981.

Raasch, J. "The Monastic Quality of Purity of Heart and its Sources." *Studia Monastica* 12 (1970).

Rinpoche, Sogyal. *The Tibetan Book of Living and Dying*. San Francisco: Harper, 1992.

Rousseau, P. *Ascetics, Authority and the Church in the Age of Jerome and Cassian*. Berkeley: University of California Press, 1985.

———.*Pachomius: The Making of a Community in Fourth Century Egypt*. Berkeley: University of California Press, 1985.

Russell, Norman, trans. *The Lives of Desert Fathers*. Introduction by Benedicta Ward. Kalamazoo, MI: Cistercian Publications, 1981.

Stewart, Columba, trans. *The World of the Desert Fathers*. Fairacres, Oxford: SLG Press, 1986.

Strand, Clark. *The Wooden Bowl*. New York: Hyperion, 1998.

Suzuki, Shunryu. *Not Always So*. New York: Harper Collins, 2002.

Swan, Laura. *The Forgotten Desert Mothers*. New York: Paulist Press, 2001.

Waddell, Helen. *The Desert Fathers*. Ann Arbor: The University of Michigan Press, 1957.

Ward, Benedicta. *Harlots of the Desert*. Kalamazoo, MI: Cistercian Publications, 1987.

———. trans. *The Sayings of the Desert Fathers: The Alphabetical Collection*. Kalamazoo, MI: Cistercian Publications, 1975.

———. trans. *The Wisdom of the Desert Fathers*. Fairacres, Oxford: SLG Press, 1986.

Wicks, Robert J. *Touching the Holy*. Notre Dame, IN: Ave Maria Press, 1992.

Apprenticeship

Albom, Mitch. *Tuesdays with Morrie: An Old Man, Young Man, and Life's Greatest Lessons*. New York: Doubleday, 1997.

Barry, William A. and Connolly, William J. *The Practice of Spiritual Direction*. San Francisco: Harper, 1982.

Brach, Tara. *Radical Acceptance*. New York: Bantam, 2003.

Brazier, Donald. *Zen Therapy*. New York: Wiley, 1997.

Chadwick, David. *Crooked Cucumber: The Life and Zen Teachings of Shunryu Suzuki*. New York: Broadway, 1999.

Chödrön, Pema. *When Things Fall Apart: Transcending the Sorrows of the Human Mind*. Boston: Shambhala, 1997.

Cousineau, Phil. *The Art of Pilgrimage*. San Francisco: Conari Press, 1998.

Crane, George. *Bones of the Master: A Buddhist Monk's Search for the Lost Heart of China*. New York: Doubleday, 2000.

de Mello, Anthony. *One Minute Wisdom*. New York: Doubleday, 1986.

Dougherty, Rose Mary. *Group Spiritual Direction: Community for Discernment*. Mahwah, NJ: Paulist Press, 1995.

Dyckman, Katherine Mane and Carroll, L. Patrich. *Inviting the Mystic, Supporting the Prophet: An Introduction to Spiritual Direction*. Mahwah, NJ: Paulist Press, 1981.

Edwards, Tilden. *Spiritual Friend: Reclaiming the Gift of Spiritual Direction*. Mahwah, NJ: Paulist, 1980.

Harvey, Andrew. *Journey in Ladakh*. Boston: Houghton Mifflin, 1984.

Gratton, Carolyn. *The Art of Spiritual Guidance*. New York: Crossroad, 1992.

Johnson, Sandy. *The Book of Tibetan Elders: The Life Stories and Wisdom of the Great Spiritual Masters of Tibet*. New York: Riverhead, 1999.

Kornfield, Jack. *A Path with Heart*. New York: Doubleday, 1993.

———. *After the Ecstasy, the Laundry*. New York: Bantam, 2000.

Leech, Kenneth. *Soul Friend*. San Francisco: Harper, 1977.

May, Gerald. G. *Care of Mind, Care of Spirit: Psychiatric Dimensions of Spiritual Direction*. San Francisco: Harper, 1982.

Morneau, Robert. *Spiritual Direction*. Mahwah, NJ: Paulist Press, 2000.

Nouwen, Henri. *Genesee Diary: Report from a Trappist Monastery*. New York: Doubleday, 1976.

Rilke, Ranier Maria. *Letters to a Young Poet*. New York: Norton, 1954.

Rolheiser, Ronald. *The Holy Longing: A Search for a Christian Spirituality*. New York: Doubleday, 1999.

Ruffing, Janet. *Spiritual Direction*. Mahwah, NJ: Paulist Press, 2000.

Sellner, Edward C. *Mentoring: The Ministry of Spiritual Kinship*. Notre Dame, IN: Ave Maria Press, 1990.

Vanderwall, Francis. *Spiritual Directions*. Mahwah, NJ: Paulist Press, 1981.

Wicks, Robert. *Sharing Wisdom: The Practical Art of Giving and Receiving Mentoring*. New York: Crossroad, 2000.

REVIEWS FOR ROBERT WICKS' RECENT WORK
RIDING THE DRAGON (Sorin Books). . .

With life offering so many more challenges as we pursue a culture of violence, Dr. Wicks' book on how to ride the dragon instead of trying to slay it is not only timely but very effective. I recommend it wholeheartedly.

Arun Gandhi
Founder, M. K. Gandhi Institute for Nonviolence

Like a good friend's support in tough times, *Riding the Dragon* is both compassionate and wise.

Jack Kornfield
Author, *A Path with Heart*

All I had to do was read the chapter titles in this book to know that this was one dragon I wanted to ride. Wicks is a master who makes the spiritual life doable.

Sister Helen Prejean
Author, *Dead Man Walking*

The lessons . . . are easy to understand, but they also contain subtleties that make them worthwhile to contemplate. Wicks offers them in a warm and encouraging voice, which many readers will find easy to return to.

Shambala Sun

Detailed and well thought out, this book nicely blends Eastern and Western wisdom—think Don Miguel Ruiz's Toltec themed *The Four Agreements* done Zen-style.

Library Journal

More favorites from Robert J. Wicks

Touching the Holy
Ordinariness, Self-Esteem, and Friendship
Robert J. Wicks offers fresh insights into the spirit
ality and psychology of sound self-esteem and rea
friendship.

ISBN: 1-933495-02-2 / 192 pages / $12.95
Sorin Books

Riding the Dragon
10 Lessons for Inner Strength in Challenging Tim

*Like a good friend's support in tough times, **Riding the
Dragon** is both compassionate and wise.*
-Jack Kornfield
American Buddhist writer and teacher, author of *A Path with Heart*

PAPERBACK ISBN: 1-893732-94-0 / 160 pages / $12.95
HARDCOVER ISBN: 1-893732-65-7 /160 pages / $17.95
Sorin Books

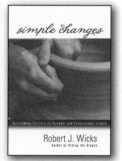

Simple Changes
*Overcoming Barriers to Personal
and Professional Growth*
This step-by-step guide offers sixteen simple yet
powerful approaches to encourage readers toward
modest, gradual changes in personal attitudes and
perspectives.

PAPERBACK ISBN: 1-933495-01-4 / 160 pages / $12.95
HARDCOVER ISBN: 0-88347-462-X / 144 pages / $15.95
Sorin Books

Available from your bookstore or from
ave maria press / Notre Dame, IN 46556
www.avemariapress.com / Ph: 800-282-1865
A Ministry of the Indiana Province of Holy Cross

Keycode: FØSØ1Ø7ØØØ